THE BOOK OF USELESS
INFORMATION

THE BOOK OF USELESS INFORMATION

BY

KEITH WATERHOUSE, RICHARD LITTLEJOHN

JOSEPH CONNOLLY, JOHN MCENTEE, NOEL BOTHAM,

BRIAN HITCHEN, MICHAEL DILLON,

ALASDAIR LONG, SUGGS ET AL

JOHN BLAKE

Published by John Blake Publishing Ltd, 3 Bramber Court,
2 Bramber Road, London W14 9PB, England

First published in paperback in 2002

ISBN 1 903402 79 4

British Library Cataloguing-in-Publication Data: A catalogue record
for this book is available from the British Library.

Design by ENVY

Printed and bound in Great Britain by Bookmarque, Ltd,
Croydon, Surrey

20 19

Papers used by John Blake Publishing Ltd are natural, recyclable
products made from wood grown in sustainable forests.
The manufacturing processes conform to the environmental

MEMBERS OF THE USELESS INFORMATION SOCIETY

NOEL BOTHAM (CHAIRMAN)

KEITH WATERHOUSE (GENERAL SECRETARY)

KENNY CLAYTON (BEADLE)

FATHER MICHAEL SEED (CHAPLAIN)

MICHAEL DILLON

BRIAN HITCHEN

ALASDAIR LONG

TIM WOODWARD

RICHARD LITTLEJOHN

STEVE WALSH

STRUAN RODGER

GAVIN HANS-HAMILTON

ASHLEY LUFF

SUGGS

MIKE MOLLOY

MICHAEL BOOTH

JOHN PAYNE

BARRY PALIN

JOSEPH CONNOLLY

TONY COBB

JOHN MCENTEE

JOHN BLAKE

JOHN ROBERTS

BILL HAGERTY

CHARLES LOWE

JOHN KING

KEN STOTT

RICHARD CORRIGAN

CONNER WALSH

JOHN TAYLOR

CONTENTS

INTRODUCTION

Oh, but just how useless is useless? There, as Shakespeare observes in Act III Scene I of *The Oxford Dictionary of Quotations*, is the rub.

For instance, the most useless fact I know is that of all the teams on the football pools coupon, Hull City is the only one whose letters cannot be shaded in by an idle doodler while awaiting the results.

Yet, hold on. This information, while eminently useless to me, could prove a boon and a blessing to the editor of the Hull City fanzine, desperate to fill his paras.

Similarly, the news that flamingos can only eat with their heads upside down, while of more than passing interest to a female flamingo teaching its fledglings to eat up their shrimp, is of little use to a human being trained to sit up at a table and employ a knife and fork. Yet suppose someone made one a present of a flamingo and it persisted in eating with its head upside down. You could spend a fortune on vets' bills before learning that, in flamingo circles, that is the way it is done.

So we have to tread carefully. There have to be checks and balances. At our Useless Information

Society summit meetings, we have these in the form of our formidable resident beadle, the distinguished jazz musician Kennie Clayton. If Mr Beadle Clayton judges that an item may be put to use in the community, he solemnly bangs his ceremonial staff and it is ruled out of order. There is no appeal, although barracking and cries of 'Rubbish!' are permitted.

An exception is sometimes made of material that may be of use to a biographer. Thus, when I learned from a newspaper cutting that Marilyn Monroe had six toes, I eagerly produced this nugget at the next Useless Information soiree in the confident belief that, with so many Marilyn biographers still trawling, it would get under the net. So it proved. What I hadn't bargained for was that one of our more pedantic members – and we have a few – would seek to have the item barred on purely arithmetical grounds, on the basis that in total she must have had eleven toes at least.

The only other transgression is that of being boring. At the society's earliest meetings, a few members misundertood the nature of uselessness and came up with such conversation-stoppers as that the Mississippi is 1171 miles long or, for those that prefer it, 1884 kilometres. We useless information aficionados are not interested in the length of rivers, a fact that is traditionally conveyed to the offender with elaborate yawns and shouts of 'Boring!' Tell us, however, that in the Nuuanu valley of Honolulu there is a river that flows upwards, and our eyes light up.

Mr Gradgrind, in the same volume as the Bard's 'There's the rub' gag, observes, 'Facts alone are wanted in life.' That is the policy of The Useless Information Society. It could be our motto.

But there are facts and facts. Useless information, as may be judged from this modest volume, is not in the same category as trivia, as in Trivial Pursuit. We do not care about any of that *Guinness Book of Records* kind of stuff. All our information has to pass the 'Not a Lot of People Know That' test, preceded by gasps of surprise and, in extreme cases, followed by wild applause.

If we can send our fellow members home with their heads reeling under the weight of a cornucopia of entirely useless and out-of-the-way facts, then our deliberations will not have been in vain.

Keith Waterhouse

FAMOUS PEOPLE

1

FAMOUS PEOPLE

Andy Garcia was a Siamese twin.

Arnold Schwarzenegger bought the first Hummer manufactured for civilian use in 1992. The vehicle weighed in at 6,300 lbs and was seven feet wide.

Arnold Schwarzenegger paid $772,500 for President John F Kennedy's golf clubs at a 1996 auction.

Jim Carrey's middle name is Eugene.

Keanu Reeves's first name means 'cool breeze over the mountains' in the Hawaiian language.

Steven Seagal is a 7th degree black belt in Aikido.

Tom Hanks is related to Abraham Lincoln.

Tommy Lee Jones and Vice-President Al Gore were freshmen roommates at Harvard.

FAMOUS PEOPLE

Robin Williams was voted in high school the least likely to succeed.

Actress Sarah Bernhardt played a 13-year-old Juliet when she was 70 years old.

Although starring in many gangster films, James Cagney started his career as a chorus boy.

As a child, Jodie Foster appeared in Coppertone commercials.

Bill Cosby was the first black man to win a best actor Emmy.

Bruce Lee was so fast that they actually had to slow down a film so you could see his moves.

Bruce Willis's real first name is Walter.

Burt Reynolds played football at Florida State University.

FAMOUS PEOPLE

Charlie Chaplin started in show business at age five.

Charlie Chaplin was so popular during the 1920s and 1930s he received over 73,000 letters in just two days during a visit to London.

Cher's given name is Cherilyn La Pierre.

Cleo and Caesar were the early stage names of Cher and Sonny Bono.

Dan Aykroyd's conehead from Saturday Night Live was auctioned off at $2,200.

David Niven and George Lazenby were the only two actors who played James Bond only once.

Harrison Ford's scar on his face was caused by a car accident.

Hulk Hogan's real name is Terry Bollea.

Ice Cube's real name is O'Shea Jackson.

FAMOUS PEOPLE

■ In 1953, Marilyn Monroe appeared as the first *Playboy* centrefold.

■ Jack Nicholson appeared in *The Andy Griffith Show* twice.

■ James Dean died in a Porsche Spydor.

■ James Doohan who plays Lt. Commander Montgomery Scott on *Star Trek* is missing his entire middle finger on his right hand.

■ Jodie Foster attended Yale University.

■ John Forsythe was the voice of the Angels' Charlie.

■ John Wayne's real birth name was Marion Morrison.

■ Judy Garland's real name was Frances Gumm.

■ Katherine Hepburn is the only actress to win four Oscars for best actress.

FAMOUS PEOPLE

■ Keanu Reeves once managed a pasta shop in Toronto.

■ Mae West did not utter her infamous line 'Is that a gun in your pocket or are you just happy to see me?' until her last film *Sextette*. It had been floating around for years and has always been attributed to her, but its exact origins are unknown.

■ Melanie Griffith's mother is actress Tippi Hedren, best known for her lead role in Alfred Hitchcock's *The Birds*.

■ Michael J Fox was born in Edmonton, AB, Canada.

■ Peter Falk, who played Columbo, has a glass eye.

■ Peter Mayhew, who played Chewbacca in the first three *Star Wars* movies, was a hospital porter in London before starring as the Wookie.

■ Roseanne Barr used to be an opening act for Julio Iglesias.

FAMOUS PEOPLE

Shirley Temple made $1 million by the age of 10.

Singer Bruce Springsteen has three kids named Sam, Evan and Jessica.

Steve Martin's first movie was *The Jerk*.

Sylvia Miles had the shortest performance ever nominated for an Oscar with *Midnight Cowboy*. Her entire role lasted only six minutes.

The first actress to appear on a postage stamp was Grace Kelly.

Tom Cruise at one time wanted to be a priest. His acting career got in the way.

Tom Cruise is a member of the Church of Scientology.

Tom Cruise's name was Thomas Mapother before he changed it.

FAMOUS PEOPLE

■ William Shatner went to Balfour Collegiate (Regina, Saskatchewan) during his high school years.

■ Al Capone's business card said he was a used furniture dealer.

■ Al Capone's famous scar (which earned him the nickname Scarface) was from an attack. The brother of a girl he had insulted attacked him with a knife, leaving him with three distinctive scars.

■ Behram, an Indian thug, holds the record for most murders by a single individual. He strangled 931 people between 1790 and 1840 with a piece of yellow and white cloth called a *ruhmal*. The most by a woman is 610, by Countess Erzsebet Bathory of Hungary.

■ Mass murderer Charles Manson recorded an album called *Lie*.

■ While in Alcatraz, Al Capone was inmate #85.

FAMOUS PEOPLE

Adolf Hitler's great-great-grandmother was a Jewish maid.

Fidel Castro was once a star baseball player for the Univeristy of Havana in the 1940s.

■ Robert Kennedy was killed in the Ambassador Hotel, the same hotel that housed Marilyn Monroe's first modelling agency.

■ Thomas Marshall (1854–1925), US Vice-President, once remarked, 'What this country needs is a good five-cent cigar.'

While at Havard University, Edward Kennedy was suspended for cheating in a Spanish exam.

William Pitt was England's youngest Prime Minister at the age of only 24, elected in 1783.

AMOUS PEOPLE

A short time before Lincoln's assassination he dreamed he was going to die, and he related his dream to the Senate.

Abraham Lincoln died in the same bed that had been occupied by his assassin John Wilkes Booth.

Abraham Lincoln had a nervous breakdown in 1836.

Abraham Lincoln had a wart on his face.

Abraham Lincoln's famous Gettysburg Address consisted of just 272 words.

Abraham Lincoln's mother died when the family dairy cow ate poisonous mushrooms and Ms Lincoln drank the milk.

All US presidents have worn glasses; some of them just didn't like to be seen with them in public.

FAMOUS PEOPLE

Andrew Jackson was the only president to believe that the world is flat.

Andrew Johnson was the only self-educated tailor. He is the only president to make his own clothes and those of his cabinet.

Before winning the election in 1860, Abraham Lincoln lost eight elections for various offices.

Bill Clinton was the first left-handed American president to serve two terms.

David Rice Atchinson was President of the United States for exactly one day.

Eamon de Valera, who was born in the US, was once president of Ireland.

Former US president Bill Clinton has a passion for chicken.

Former US president Jimmy Carter had an operation for haemorrhoids while he was in office.

AMOUS PEOPLE

Former US President Ronald Reagan once wore a Nazi uniform while acting in a film during his Hollywood days.

Former US President Ulysses S Grant had the boyhood nickname 'Useless'.

Four men were executed for Abraham Lincoln's assassination.

George Washington grew marijuana in his garden.

George Washington was deathly afraid of being buried alive. After he died, he wanted to be laid out for three days just to make sure he was dead.

George Washington's false teeth were made of whale bone.

Gerald Ford was once a male model.

Herbert Hoover was the first US president to have a telephone in his office.

FAMOUS PEOPLE

James Buchanan is said to have had the neatest handwriting of all the presidents.

James Buchanan was the only unmarried president of the US.

Jimmy Carter is a speed reader (2000 wpm).

Jimmy Carter was the first US president born in a hospital.

Louis IV of France had a stomach the size of two regular stomachs.

Louis XIV bathed once a year.

Louis XIV had 40 personal wigmakers and almost 1000 wigs.

Louisa May Alcott, author of the classic *Little Women*, hated children. She only wrote the book because her publisher asked her to.

FAMOUS PEOPLE

Lyndon B Johnson was the first president of the United States to wear contact lenses.

Most US presidents have been born in the state of Virginia.

No US president has been an only child.

Only one US president, Woodrow Wilson, has held a Ph.D. degree.

President Grover Cleveland was a draft dodger. He hired someone to enter the service in his place, for which he was ridiculed by his political opponent, James G. Blaine. It was soon discovered, however, that Blaine had done the same thing himself.

President James Garfield could write Latin with one hand and Greek with the other – simultaneously!

President John F Kennedy could read four newspapers in 20 minutes.

FAMOUS PEOPLE

President John Quincy Adams owned a pet alligator which he kept in the East Room of the White House.

President John Tyler had 15 children.

President Taft got stuck in his bathtub on his Inauguration Day and had to be pried out by his attendants.

President Taft had a special reinforced steel dining chair.

President Teddy Roosevelt died from an infected tooth.

President Theodore Roosevelt was the first to announce to the world that Maxwell House coffee is 'Good to the last drop'.

President Theodore Roosevelt wrote 37 books.

■ President Woodrow Wilson wrote all of his speeches in longhand.

FAMOUS PEOPLE

■ Richard Nixon left instructions for 'California, Here I Come' to be the last piece of music played (slowly and softly) were he to die in office.

■ Richard Nixon's favourite drink was a dry martini.

■ Ronald Reagan married his first wife, Jane Wyman, at Forest Lawn Cemetery in Glendale, California.

■ Ronald Reagan sent out the army photographer who first discovered Marilyn Monroe.

■ Ronald Reagan was the only divorced president.

■ Roosevelt was the most superstitious president – he travelled continually but never left on a Friday. He also would not sit at the same table that held 13 other people.

FAMOUS PEOPLE

The annual White House Easter egg-roll was started by US President Hayes in 1878.

The first US president to be inaugurated in Washington, DC was Thomas Jefferson.

■ The first US president to visit Moscow was Richard Nixon.

■ The longest inaugural address by a US president was given by William Henry Harrison. It was one hour and 45 minutes long during an intense snowstorm. One month later he died of pneumonia.

The only president to be head of a labour union was Ronald Reagan.

The only three US presidents who ever had to deal with real or impending impeachment – Andrew Johnson, Richard Nixon and Bill Clinton – all have names that are euphemisms for penis – johnson, dick and willie.

FAMOUS PEOPLE

■ Theodore Roosevelt finished a speech he was delivering after being shot in the chest, before he accepted any medical help in 1812.

■ Theodore Roosevelt's mother and first wife died on the same day in 1884.

■ There has never been a president from the Air Force or Marine Corps, although Reagan was in the Army Air Corps.

■ Thomas Jefferson anonymously submitted design plans for the White House. They were rejected.

■ Thomas Jefferson, John Adams and James Monroe all died on 4 July. Jefferson and Adams died at practically the same minute of the same day.

■ US President Millard Fillmore's mother feared he may have been mentally retarded.

FAMOUS PEOPLE

■ When the First Lady Eleanor Roosevelt received an alarming number of threatening letters soon after her husband became President at the height of the Depression, the Secret Service insisted that she carry a pistol in her purse.

■ All 17 children of Queen Anne died before she did.

■ Anne Boleyn, Queen Elizabeth I's mother, had six fingers on one hand.

■ Catherine the Great relaxed by being tickled.

■ Elizabeth I suffered from anthophobia (a fear of roses).

■ Elizabeth Taylor has appeared on the cover of *Life* magazine more than anyone else.

■ George Washington had to borrow money to go to his own inauguration.

FAMOUS PEOPLE

King Tut's tomb contained *four* coffins. The third coffin was made from 2,500 pounds of gold. And in today's market is worth approximately $13,000,000.

Six of Queen Victoria's grandchildren were married to rulers of countries – England, Russia, Germany, Sweden, Norway and Romania.

One of Queen Victoria's children gave her a bustle for Christmas that played 'God Save the Queen' when she sat down.

Prince Harry and Prince William are uncircumcised.

Princess Anne competed in the 1976 Summer Olympics.

Princess Grace of Monaco was once on the board of 20th Century-Fox.

Queen Berengaria (1191 AD) of England never lived in or visited England.

FAMOUS PEOPLE

Queen Elizabeth I was good friends with William Shakespeare.

Queen Victoria eased the discomfort of her menstrual cramps by having her doctor supply her with marijuana.

Queen Victoria's mother – tongue was German.

The first thing Queen Victoria did after her coronation was to remove her bed from her mother's room.

The Queen of England has two birthdays – one real and one official.

The royal house of Saudi Arabia has close to 10,000 princes and princesses.

The shortest British monarch was Charles I, who was 4'9.

While performing her duties as queen, Cleopatra sometimes wore a fake beard.

FAMOUS PEOPLE

According to Elvis's autopsy, he had ten different drugs in his body at the time of his death.

Al Kooper played keyboards for Bob Dylan before he was famous.

Elvis Presley had a twin brother named Garon, who died at birth, which is why Elvis's middle name was spelled Aron, in honour of his brother.

Elvis Presley loved to eat meatloaf.

Elvis Presley failed his music class in school.

Elvis Presley never gave an encore.

Elvis Presley received his US army discharge on 5 March, 1960.

Elvis Presley's favourite food was fried peanut butter and banana sandwiches.

FAMOUS PEOPLE

Elvis Presley was once appointed Special Agent of the Bureau of Narcotics and Dangerous Drugs.

Elvis Presley weighed 230 pounds at the time of his death.

Frank Sinatra was once quoted as saying that rock 'n' roll was only played by 'cretinous goons'.

Jim Morrison (from the rock group The Doors) was the first rock star to be arrested on stage.

Jimi Hendrix, Janis Joplin and Jim Morrison were all 27 years old when they died.

Karen Carpenter's doorbell chimed the first six notes of 'We've Only Just Begun'.

Madonna once did a commercial for Pepsi.

Michael Jackson is black.

AMOUS PEOPLE

Mick Jagger attended the London School of Economics for two years.

Paul McCartney and Ringo Starr were left handed.

Paul McCartney's mother was a midwife.

Shannon Hoon, the late lead singer of the group Blind Melon was a back-up singer for Guns N' Roses on their *Use Your Illusion 1* CD.

Sheryl Crow's two front teeth are fake. She knocked them out when she tripped on stage earlier in her career.

The opera singer Enrico Caruso practised in the bath, while accompanied by a pianist in a nearby room.

Tina Turner's real name is Annie Mae Bullock.

Vanilla Ice's real name is Robert Van Winkle.

WORLD OF ANIMALS

WORLD OF ANIMALS

A baby platypus remains blind after birth for 11 weeks.

A barnacle has the largest penis of any other animal in relation to its size.

A blind chameleon still changes colour to match its environment.

A camel's backbone is just as straight as a horse's.

A chameleon's tongue is twice the length of its body.

A crocodile's tongue is attached to the roof of its mouth.

Deer cannot eat hay.

A donkey will sink in quicksand but a mule won't.

A dragonfly has a lifespan of four to seven weeks.

A duck has three eyelids.

WORLD OF ANIMALS

A female ferret will die if it goes on heat and cannot find a mate.

A geep is a cross between a goat and a sheep.

A group of finches is called a charm.

A group of frogs is called an army.

A group of geese on the ground is called a gaggle; a group of geese in the air is a skein.

A group of goats is called a trip.

A group of hares is called a husk.

A group of kangaroos is called a mob.

A group of owls is called a parliament.

A group of rhinos is called a crash.

A group of toads is called a knot.

WORLD OF ANIMALS

A hedgehog's heart beats 300 times a minute on average.

A jackrabbit can jump as high as 15 feet.

A large swarm of locusts can eat 80,000 tons of corn in a day.

A male chimpanzee is five times hornier than the average human.

A mole can dig over 250 feet of tunnel in a single night.

A rat can last longer without water than a camel.

A rhinoceros's horn is made of compacted hair.

A rodent's teeth never stop growing. They are worn down by the animal's constant gnawing on bark, leaves and other vegetables.

WORLD OF ANIMALS

■ A scallop has a total of 35 eyes which are all blue.

■ A sheep, a duck and a rooster were the first passengers in a hot air balloon.

■ A shrimp has more than a hundred pairs of chromosomes in each cell nucleus.

■ A single sheep's fleece might well contain as many as 26 million fibres.

■ A species of Australian dragonfly has been clocked at 36mph.

■ A species of earthworm in Australia grows up to 10 feet in length.

■ A square mile of fertile earth has 32 million earthworms in it.

■ A squirrel cannot contract or carry the rabies virus.

■ A strand from the web of the golden spider is as strong as a steel wire of the same size.

WORLD OF ANIMALS

A woodchuck breathes 2,100 times an hour, but it only breathes 10 times an hour while it is hibernating.

According to Dr David Gems, a British geneticist, sex-craved male mice, who spend five to 11 hours per day pursuing female mice, could live years longer if they abstained.

After eating, the housefly regurgitates its food and eats it again.

All porcupines float in water.

Alligators cannot move backwards.

An estimated 80 per cent of creatures on earth have six legs.

An iguana can stay under water for 28 minutes.

An octopus will eat its own arms if it gets really hungry.

WORLD OF ANIMALS

An ostrich's eye is bigger than its brain.

Anteaters prefer termites to ants.

Any female bee in a beehive could have been the queen if she had been fed the necessary royal jelly. All female bees in a given hive are sisters.

Apart from humans, certain species of chimpanzee are the only animals to experiment sexually. They have been known to 'wife swap' and indulge in group sex.

At birth a panda is smaller than a mouse and weighs about four ounces.

Basilisks are frequently called Jesus Christ Lizards because of their ability to run on water.

Bats always turn left when exiting a cave.

Bats are the only mammals that can fly.

WORLD OF ANIMALS

■ Bats can live up to 30 years or more.

■ Bees do not have ears.

■ Bees have five eyes. There are three small eyes on the top of a bee's head and two larger ones in front.

■ Belize is the only country in the world with a jaguar reserve.

■ Between 1902 and 1907 the same tiger killed 436 people in India.

■ Boanthropy is a disease in which a man thinks he's an ox.

■ Bulls are colourblind and will usually charge at a moving cape regardless of colour.

■ Butterflies taste with their hind feet.

■ Carnivorous animals will not eat another animal that has been hit by a lightning strike.

WORLD OF ANIMALS

Caterpillars have about 4,000 muscles. Humans, by comparison, have only about 600.

Cats have over 100 vocal sounds, while dogs only have about 10.

Cattle are the only mammals that are retro-mingent (they urinate backwards).

Certain fireflies emit a light so penetrating that it can pass through flesh and wood.

Certain frogs can be frozen solid, then thawed, and continue living.

Certain species of male butterflies produce scents that serve in attracting females during courtship.

A cockroach's favourite food is the glue on the back of stamps.

During its lifetime an oyster changes its sex from male to female and back several times.

WORLD OF ANIMALS

Eagles can live in captivity for up to 46 years.

Estuarine crocodiles are the biggest of all 26 species of the crocodilian family.

Every single hamster in the US today comes from a single litter captured in Syria in 1930.

Flamingos are pink because they consume vast quantities of algae.

Flamingos can live up to 80 years.

Flamingos can only eat with their heads upside down.

Frog-eating bats identify edible from poisonous frogs by listening to the mating calls of male frogs. Frogs counter by hiding and using short, difficult to locate calls.

Frogs drink and breathe through their skin.

WORLD OF ANIMALS

Frogs move faster than toads.

Frogs must close their eyes to swallow.

Fur seals get miserably sick when they're carried aboard ships.

Giant flying foxes that live in Indonesia have wingspans of nearly six feet.

Giant squids have eyes as big as watermelons.

Giant tortoises can live to be 150 years old or older.

Golden toads are so rare that a biological reserve has been specifically created for them.

Gorillas beat their chests when they get nervous.

Gorillas often sleep for up to 14 hours a day.

WORLD OF ANIMALS

Grasshoppers have white blood.

Herons have been observed to drop insects on the water and then catch the fish that surface for the bugs.

Hippopotami cannot swim.

Human birth control pills work on gorillas.

If a frog's mouth is held open for too long the frog will suffocate.

Iguanas, koalas and Komodo dragons all have two penises.

In 1859, 24 rabbits were released in Australia. Within six years the population grew to two million.

In 1978, more deer were killed by Connecticut automobile drivers than by Connecticut hunters.

WORLD OF ANIMALS

In Miami, Florida, roosting vultures have taken to snatching poodles from rooftop patios.

In Michigan, USA, it is illegal to chain an alligator to a fire hydrant.

In the past 60 years, the groundhog has only predicted the weather correctly 28 per cent of the time. The rushing back and forth from burrows is believed to indicate sexual activity, not shadow seeking.

It is estimated that millions of trees are planted by forgetful squirrels.

It is physically impossible for pigs to look up in the sky.

It takes 12,000 head of cattle to produce one pound of adrenaline.

It takes a sloth two weeks to digest the food it eats.

WORLD OF ANIMALS

It was discovered on a space mission that a frog can throw up. The frog throws up its stomach first, so the stomach is dangling out of its mouth. Then the frog uses its forearms to dig out all of the stomach's contents and then swallows the stomach back down.

Jackals have one more pair of chromosomes than dogs or wolves.

Jackrabbits can reach a speed of 50 miles per hour and can leap as high as five feet.

Jaguars are scared of dogs.

Japan is the largest exporter of frogs' legs.

Lorne Green had one of his nipples bitten off by an alligator while host of *Lorne Green's Wild Kingdom*.

WORLD OF ANIMALS

Male bees will try to attract sex partners with orchid fragrance.

Man and the two-toed sloth are the only land animals that typically mate face to face.

Many hamsters only blink one eye at a time.

Mexican free-tailed bats sometimes fly up to two miles high to feed or to catch tail-winds that carry them over long distances at speeds of more than 60 miles per hour.

Mice will nurse babies that are not their own.

Mice, whales, elephants, giraffes and man all have seven neck vertebrae.

Mongooses were brought to Hawaii to kill rats. This plan failed because rats are nocturnal while the mongoose hunts during the day.

WORLD OF ANIMALS

Moose have very poor vision. Some have even tried to mate with cars.

More than a third of the field mice in the Kesterson National Wildlife refuge near Los Banos, California have both male and female reproductive organs.

Most published species of dinosaurs have been published within the last 20 years.

Mountain goats are not goats. They are small antelopes.

Next to man, the porpoise is the most intelligent creature on earth.

No pearls of value are ever found in North American oysters.

One species of antelope, the Sitatunga, can sleep under water.

WORLD OF ANIMALS

■ Only 30 per cent of the famous Maryland blue crab are actually from Maryland, the rest are from North Carolina and Virginia.

■ Orangutans warn people to stay out of their territory by belching.

■ Parthenogenesis is the term used to describe the process by which certain animals are able to reproduce themselves in successive female generations without intervention of a male of the species. At least one species of lizard is known to do so.

■ Penguins do not tip over when a airplane flies over them.

■ Porcupines are excellent swimmers, because their quills are hollow.

■ Rats can't vomit.

■ Reindeer like to eat bananas.

WORLD OF ANIMALS

Research indicates that mosquitoes are attracted to people who have recently eaten bananas.

Rhinos are in the same family as horses, and are thought to have inspired the myth of the unicorn.

Roosters cannot crow if they can't fully extend their necks.

Sea otters have two coats of fur.

■ Seals must teach their young how to swim.

Slugs have four noses.

Small cockroaches are more likely to die on their backs than large cockroaches.

Some dinosaurs were as small as hens.

Some ribbon worms will eat themselves if they cannot find food.

WORLD OF ANIMALS

Southern Indian drug addicts get high by having venomous snakes bite their tongues. This can give addicts a 16-hour high, but can be very deadly.

Tarantulas cannot spin webs.

Tarantulas do not use muscles to move their legs. They control the amount of blood pumped into them to extend and retract their legs.

The candlefish is so oily that it was once burned for fuel.

The average cost of rehabilitating a seal after the Exxon Valdez oil spill in Alaska was $80,000.

The average garden variety caterpillar has 248 muscles in its head.

The average porcupine has more than 30,000 quills.

WORLD OF ANIMALS

■ The beautiful but deadly Australian sea wasp (Chironex fleckeri) is the most venomous jellyfish in the world. Its cardio toxic venom has caused the deaths of 66 people off the coast of Queensland since 1880, with victims dying within one to three minutes if medical aid is not available.

■ The brown myotis bat's young when born are equivalent to a woman giving birth to a 30lb baby.

■ The adult electric eel has enough electrical power in it to power a house of about 1,200 square feet.

■ The cells which make up the antlers of a moose are the fastest growing animal cells in nature.

■ The cheetah can reach a speed of up to 45 miles per hour in only two seconds.

■ The colour of a yak's milk is pink.

WORLD OF ANIMALS

The deepest penguin dive was 1261ft under the water.

The electric eel has an average discharge of 400 volts.

The elephant is the only mammal that can't jump.

The female ferret is referred to as a jill.

The giant cricket of Africa enjoys eating human hair.

The goose was the first domesticated animal.

The guinea pig originated in South America.

The hippopotamus is the hog's largest living relative.

The honey badger can withstand hundreds of African bee stings that would kill any other animal.

WORLD OF ANIMALS

■ The Kansas City Railroad use to stop their trains, in 1868, to allow the passengers to shoot at passing buffalo.

■ The Latin name for moose is *alces alces*.

■ The leg bones of a bat are so thin that no bat can walk.

■ The lifespan of a squirrel is about nine years.

■ The longest recorded life span of a camel was 35 years, five months.

■ The longest species of centipede is the giant scolopender *(Scolopendra gigantea)*, found in the rain forests of Central and South America. It has 23 segments (46 legs) and specimens have been measured up to 10.5 inches long and one inch in diameter.

WORLD OF ANIMALS

■ The longest species of earthworm is the Megascolides australis, found in Australia in 1868. An average specimen measures 4 feet in length, 2 feet when contracted, and 7 feet when naturally extended.

■ The male gypsy moth can smell the virgin female gypsy moth from eight miles away.

■ The Nile and Indo-Pacific saltwater crocodiles are the only two crocodiles that are considered true man-eaters.

■ The octopus's testicles are located in its head.

■ The only continent without reptiles or snakes is Antarctica.

■ The only female animal that has antlers is the caribou.

■ The only purple animal is the South African Blesbok.

WORLD OF ANIMALS

The original name for butterfly was the flutterby.

The poison arrow frog has enough poison to kill about 2,200 people.

The poisonous copperhead smells like fresh cut cucumbers.

The Portuguese Man-of-War 'jellyfish' tentacles have been known to grow a mile in length, catching anything in its path by stinging its prey.

The pupil of an octopus's eye is rectangular.

The Quahog clam is the longest living animal, with a maximum age of up to 200 years old.

The Queen (or more precisely the Royal Household) owns all swans in England. The post of Royal Swankeeper is a post that has been around since 1215 and he and his staff are responsible for keeping accurate statistics about the number and whereabouts of the royal swans.

WORLD OF ANIMALS

The scientific name for a gorilla is 'gorilla gorilla gorilla'.

The shrimp's heart is in its head.

The tuatara lizard of New Zealand has three eyes – two in the centre of its head and one on top.

The tuatara's metabolism is so slow they only have to breathe once an hour.

The typical laboratory mouse runs five miles per night on its treadmill.

The Weddell seal can travel under water for seven miles without surfacing for air.

The woolly mammoth, extinct since the Ice Age, had tusks almost 16 feet long.

The word alligator comes from 'El Lagarto' which is Spanish for 'The Lizard.'

The world camel population is 19,627,000.

WORLD OF ANIMALS

The world's smallest mammal is the bumblebee bat of Thailand, weighing less than a penny.

The zorilla is the smelliest animal on the planet. Its anal glands can be smelled from half a mile away.

There are an average of 50,000 spiders per acre in green areas.

There have been over 1,500 documented sightings of Bigfoot since 1958.

There is no record of a non-rabid wolf attack on a human.

Tigers have striped skin, not just striped fur.

To escape the grip of a crocodile's jaws, push your thumbs into its eyeballs – it will let you go instantly.

To keep cool, ostriches urinate on their legs; it then evaporates like sweat.

WORLD OF ANIMALS

■ To keep from being separated while sleeping, sea otters tie themselves together with kelp, often drifting miles out to sea during the night.

■ To see at night as well as an owl, you would need eyeballs as big as a grapefruit.

■ Toads don't have teeth, but frogs do.

■ When angered, the Tazmanian devil turns pinkish-red.

■ When cornered, the horned toad shoots blood from its eyes.

■ When young, black sea basses are mostly female, but at the age of five many switch sex and become male.

■ Woodpecker scalps, porpoise teeth and giraffe tails have all been used as money.

WORLD OF ANIMALS

Worldwide, bats are the most important natural enemies of night-flying insects.

You can cut up a starfish into pieces and each piece will grow into a completely new starfish. .

A baby beaver stays with it parents for a period of two years

An armadillo can walk under water.

Armadillos are the only animal besides humans that can get leprosy.

Armadillos can be house broken.

■ Armadillos have four babies at a time, and they are always the same sex.

Polar bears have more problems with overheating than they do with cold. Even in very cold weather, they quickly overheat when they try to run.

Camel's milk does not curdle.

WORLD OF ANIMALS

■ Camels have three eyelids to protect their eyes from blowing sand.

It can take a deep-sea clam up to 100 years to reach 0.3 inches (8 millimetres) in length. The clam is among the slowest growing, yet longest living species on the planet.

■ Despite its reputation for being finicky, the average cat consumes about 127,750 calories a year, nearly 28 times its own weight in food and the same amount again in liquids. In case you were wondering, cats cannot survive on a vegetarian diet.

It is estimated that a single toad may catch and eat as many as 10,000 insects in the course of a summer.

It is estimated that manatees live a maximum of 50 to 60 years.

WORLD OF ANIMALS

■ Developed in Egypt about 5,000 years ago, the greyhound breed was known before the ninth century in England, where it was bred by aristocrats to hunt such small game as hares.

■ It is the female lion who does more than 90 per cent of the hunting, while the male is afraid to risk his life, or simply prefers to rest.

■ Dinosaurs lived on earth for around 165 million years before they became extinct.

■ It may take longer than two days for a chick to break out of its shell.

■ Dinosaurs were among the most sophisticated animals that ever lived on earth. They survived for nearly 150 million years – 75 times longer than humans have now lived on earth.

WORLD OF ANIMALS

It seems to biologists that, unlike their humpback whale relatives whose under water song evolves from year to year, killer whales retain individual dialects unchanged over long periods, possibly even for life.

■ Disc-winged bats of Latin America have adhesive discs on both wings and feet that enable them to live in unfurling banana leaves (or even walk up a window pane!).

It takes 11 truckloads of wood to make a proper funeral pyre for a full-size elephant.

It takes 24 hours for a tiny newborn swan to peck its way out of its shell.

■ A newly hatched crocodile is three times as large as the egg from which it has emerged.

WORLD OF ANIMALS

A 'winkle' is an edible sea snail.

A 42-foot sperm whale has about seven tons of oil in it.

A four-inch-long abalone can grip a rock with a force of 400 pounds. Two grown men are incapable of prying it loose.

A baby baleen whale depends on a mother's milk diet for at least six months.

A baby bat is called a pup.

A baby blue whale is 25 feet long at birth.

A baby caribou is so swift it can easily outrun its mother when it is only three days old.

It takes 42 days for an ostrich egg to hatch.

WORLD OF ANIMALS

A baby giraffe is about six feet tall at birth.

It takes a lobster approximately seven years to grow to be one pound

A baby grey whale drinks enough milk to fill more than 2,000 bottles a day.

It takes about 50 hours for a snake to digest one frog.

Dogs that do not tolerate small children well are the St Bernard, the Old English sheep dog, the Alaskan malamute, the bull terrier and the toy poodle.

It takes an average of 345 squirts to yield a gallon of milk from a cow's udder.

It takes approximately 69,000 venom extractions from the coral snake to fill a one-pint container.

WORLD OF ANIMALS

■ Dolphins do not breathe automatically, as humans do, and so they do not sleep as humans do. If they become unconscious, they would sink to the bottom of the sea. Without the oxygen they need to take in periodically, they would die.

■ It takes the deep-sea clam 100 years to grow to a length of one-third inch.

■ Dolphins have killed sharks by ramming them with their snouts.

■ It would require an average of 18 hummingbirds to weigh in at one ounce.

■ Dolphins jump out of the water to conserve energy. It is easier to move through the air than through the water.

WORLD OF ANIMALS

■ It's been noted that the gender of a sea turtle is determined by the temperature of the sand during egg incubation. Warm temperatures (greater than 29°C) produce more females; cooler temperatures (less than 29°C) produce more males.

■ Dolphins swim in circles while they sleep with the eye on the outside of the circle open to keep watch for predators. After a certain amount of time, they reverse and swim in the opposite direction with the opposite eye open.

■ Jackrabbits are powerful jumpers. A 20-inch adult can leap 20 feet in a single bound.

■ Domesticated turkeys (farm-raised) cannot fly. Wild turkeys can fly for short distances at up to 55 miles per hour. Wild turkeys are also fast on the ground, running at speeds of up to 30 miles per hour.

WORLD OF ANIMALS

Javelina herds require a territory of at least one square mile.

Ducks will lay eggs only in the early morning.

■ Due to a retinal adaptation that reflects light back to the retina, the night vision of tigers is six times better than that of humans.

■ During the 1800s, swan skins were used to make European ladies' powder puffs and swan feathers were used to adorn fashionable hats.

Racehorses have been known to wear out new shoes in one race.

Rats can swim for a half mile without resting, and they can tread water for three days straight.

WORLD OF ANIMALS

■ Rattlesnakes gather in groups to sleep through the winter. Sometimes up to 1,000 of them will coil up together to keep warm.

■ Reaching sexual maturity in the wild at around 15 to 20 years of age, sturgeon can live as long as 100 years. Mature females will produce millions of eggs every two to three years.

■ Just like people, mother chimpanzees often develop lifelong relationships with their offspring.

■ Red bats that live in tree foliage throughout most of North America can withstand body temperatures as low as 23°F during winter hibernation.

■ Kangaroo rats never drink water. Like their relatives the pocket mice, they carry their own water source within them, producing fluids from the food they eat and the air they breathe.

WORLD OF ANIMALS

■ During the mating season, male porcupines bristle their quills at each other and chatter their teeth in rage before attacking. All porcupines at this time become very vocal: grunting, whining, chattering, even barking and mewing at each other.

■ Reindeer have scent glands between their hind toes. The glands help them leave scent trails for the herd. Researchers say the odour smells cheesy.

■ Kangaroos can move as fast as 30 miles per hour and can leap up to 25 feet in the air.

■ Duroc is one American breed of hardy hog having drooping ears – it was allegedly named after the horse owned by the hog's breeder.

■ Reportedly, beavers mate for life.

WORLD OF ANIMALS

■ Kangaroos usually give birth to one young annually. The young kangaroo, or joey, is born alive at a very immature stage, when it is only about 2cm long and weighs less than a gram.

■ Each day, 100 or more whales are killed by fishermen.

■ Reptiles are never slimy. Their scales have few glands, and are usually silky to the touch.

■ Kittens are born both blind and deaf, but the vibration of their mother's purring is a physical signal that the kittens can feel – it acts like a homing device, signalling them to nurse.

■ Each eye of the chameleon is independent of the other. The lizard can watch and study two totally different pictures at the same time.

WORLD OF ANIMALS

■ Kittens can clock an amazing 31 miles per hour at full speed, and can cover about three times their body length per leap.

■ Eagles mate while airborne.

■ Researchers have determined that the elephant seals off the Baja coast dive deeper than whales – sometimes as deep as a mile.

■ Koalas and humans are the only animals with unique prints. Koala prints cannot be distinguished from human fingerprints.

■ Earlier penguins were capable of flight.

■ Koalas are marsupials, not bears. They also have no tail or eyelids.

■ Electric eels are not really eels but a kind of fish. Although they look like eels, their internal organs are arranged differently.

WORLD OF ANIMALS

■ Rome has more homeless cats per square mile than any other city in the world.

■ Komodo dragons eat deer and wild boar.

■ Lanolin, an essential ingredient of many expensive cosmetics, is, in its native form, a foul-smelling, waxy, tarlike substance extracted from the fleece of sheep.

■ Running in short bursts, the cheetah can reach a speed of 62 miles per hour (100 kilometres per hour).

■ Lassie, the TV collie, first appeared in a 1930s short novel entitled *Lassie Come Home* written by Eric Mowbray Knight. The dog in the novel was based on Knight's real-life collie, Toots.

■ Lemon sharks grow a new set of teeth every two weeks. They grow more than 24,000 new teeth every year.

WORLD OF ANIMALS

■ Elephants and short-tailed shrews get by on only two hours of sleep a day.

■ Schools of South American (Pacific) Humboldt squid, which reach 12 feet in length, have been known to strip 500lb marlins to the bone.

■ Like cows, snakes cannot activate their vitamin D without the presence of sunlight.

■ Elephants communicate in sound waves below the frequency that humans can hear.

■ Scientific researchers say promiscuous species of monkeys appear to have stronger immune systems than less sexually active ones.

■ Elephants have been known to remain standing after they die.

WORLD OF ANIMALS

■ Scientists say that pigs, unlike all other domestic animals, arrive at solutions by thinking them through. Pigs can be – and have been – taught to accomplish almost any feat a dog can master, and usually in a shorter period of time.

■ Like the swiftest of all antelopes, the impala can easily leap as far as 35 feet.

■ Elephants perform greeting ceremonies when a member of the group returns after a long time away. The welcoming animals spin around, flap their ears and trumpet.

■ Lions are the only truly social cat species, and usually every female in a pride, ranging from five to 30 individuals, is closely related.

■ Lions sleep up to 20 hours a day.

WORLD OF ANIMALS

Eleven chinchillas were brought from the Andes Mountains in South America in the 1930s. All chinchillas presently in North America are descended from these eleven chinchillas.

■ Scientists still know very little about the giant squid, except what can be gleaned from the carcasses of about 100 beached squid dating back to 1639. Despite centuries of myths and exciting tales of sightings of giant squid, more information is known about dinosaurs.

Sea otters have the world's densest fur – a million hairs per square inch.

Sea otters inhabit water but never get wet because they have two coats of fur.

■ Llamas are reported to be inquisitive, friendly animals. A llama greeting is marked by softly blowing on each other. According to animal experts, a soft blow to a person is the llama's way of saying hello.

WORLD OF ANIMALS

■ Sea sponges are used in drugs for treating asthma and cancer.

■ Lobsters moult 20 to 30 times before reaching the one-pound market size.

■ Seabirds have salt-excreting organs above their eyes which enable them to drink salty water; seasnakes have a similar filter at the base of their tongue.

■ Lobsters, like grasshoppers, feel no pain. They have a decentralised nervous system with no cerebral cortex, which in humans is where a reaction to painful stimuli proceeds.

■ Seals and whales keep warm in the icy polar water thanks to a layer of fat called blubber under their skin. Whale blubber can reach up to 20 inches (50 centimetres) thick.

■ Seals can sleep under water and surface for air without even waking.

WORLD OF ANIMALS

■ Lungless salamanders are the largest group of salamanders. They have no lungs or gills and breathe through their skin, which must be kept damp to allow oxygen in. If they dry out, they will die of suffocation.

■ Seals can withstand water pressure of up to 850 pounds per square inch.

■ Macaws are the largest and most colourful species of the parrot family.

■ Seals have back flippers that can't bend under the body in order to walk on land, while sea lions use their leg-like hind flippers to 'walk' on land.

■ Sharks and rays are the only animals known to man that cannot succumb to cancer. Scientists believe this is related to the fact that they have no bone – only cartilage.

WORLD OF ANIMALS

■ Several poison-dart frog species are bred at the National Aquarium in Baltimore. There, researchers gauge the toxicity of poisonous species by taste. No danger is posed, because frogs caught in the wild gradually become less poisonous, and captive offspring are nontoxic. The change may be due to diet. The frog's natural menu – mostly tropical ants and springtails – cannot be duplicated in a terrarium.

■ Male boars form harems.

■ Sharks can be dangerous even before they are born. Scientist Stewart Springer was bitten by a sand tiger shark embryo while he was examining its pregnant mother.

■ Male cockatoos can be taught to speak, but females can only chirp and sing.

■ Sharks can travel up to 40 miles per hour.

WORLD OF ANIMALS

Sharks' fossil records date back more than twice as long as that of the dinosaurs.

Male monkeys lose the hair on their heads in the same manner men do.

Sharks have a sixth sense which enables them to detect bioelectrical fields radiated by other sea creatures and to navigate by sensing changes in the earth's magnetic field.

Male sea lions may have more than 100 wives and sometimes go three months without eating.

Male western fence lizards do push-ups on tree limbs as a courtship display for females.

Shrimp swim backwards.

Mallard nests are sometimes built at a height of 40 feet above ground. Surprisingly, when leaving their nests for the first time, chicks are very rarely hurt after falling to the ground.

WORLD OF ANIMALS

■ The dodo, extinct less than 100 years after being discovered by the Dutch in 1598, was not a prolific species. The female laid just one egg a year.

■ The dog and the turkey were the only two domesticated animals in ancient Mexico.

■ The domestic cat is the only species able to hold its tail vertically while walking. Wild cats hold their tail horizontally, or tucked between their legs while walking.

■ Sidewinders are snakes that move by looping their bodies up in the air and pushing against the ground when they land. Their tracks in the ground would look like a series of straight lines angling in the direction the snake was travelling.

■ The duckbill platypus of Australia can store up to 600 worms in its large cheek pouches.

WORLD OF ANIMALS

■ Many seabirds that swallow fishes too large for immediate digestion go about with the oesophagus filled. Apparently without discomfort, the tail of the fish sticks out of the bird's mouth.

■ The Egyptian vulture, a white bird about the size of a raven, throws stones with its beak to open ostrich eggs to eat. This bird is one of the very few animals that, like man, manipulates objects as tools.

■ The electric eel has thousands of electric cells running up and down its tail. Vital body organs, such as the heart, are packed into a small space behind the head. They use their electric sense to 'see'. Their electric sensors act like radar. They send out weak impulses which bounce off objects.

■ Skunks have more than smell to protect themselves. They can withstand five times the snake venom that would kill a rabbit.

WORLD OF ANIMALS

■ Many types of fish – called mouthbrooders – carry their eggs in their mouths until the babies hatch and can care for themselves.

■ The electric eel is the most shocking animal on earth – no other animal packs such a big charge. If attacking a large prey, a nine-foot-long eel can discharge about 800 volts. One zap could stun a human. The larger the eel, the bigger the charge.

■ Snakes do not have eyelids, so even when they're asleep they cannot close their eyes. They do have a protective layer of clear scales, called brille, over their eyes.

■ Marine iguanas, saltwater crocodiles, sea snakes and sea turtles are the only surviving seawater-adapted reptiles.

■ Snakes do not urinate. They secrete and excrete uric acid, which is a solid, chalky, usually white substance.

WORLD OF ANIMALS

■ So that it can pull its lithe body into a tight, prickly little ball for defence, the hedgehog has a large muscle running along its stomach.

■ Measuring about eight feet at birth, killer whale bulls can grow to 25 feet and weigh as much as six tons.

■ The electric organs in an electric eel make up four-fifths of its body.

■ The elephant seal is the heaviest seal in the world; males can reach 21 feet (six metres) in length and 8,800 pounds.

■ Deer like to eat marijuana.

■ The elephant's closest relative is the hyrax, which is found in the Middle East and Africa and is only about one foot long. Like its gigantic cousin, the hyrax has hoofed toes and a two-chambered stomach for digesting a vegetable diet.

WORLD OF ANIMALS

■ Some bullfrogs pretend to be dead when captured, but quickly hop away when let go.

■ The emperor penguin is the largest type of penguin. It is also the deepest diver, reaching depths of 870 feet (260 metres) and staying there for up to 18 minutes.

■ Mice, whales, elephants, giraffes and humans all have seven neck vertebra.

■ The emu is Australia's largest bird at a height of seven feet tall. It can't fly, but it can swim and has the ability to run up to 40 miles per hour.

■ Migrating geese fly in a V-formation to conserve energy. A goose's wings churn the air and leave an air current behind. In the flying wedge, each bird is in position to get a lift from the current left by the bird ahead. It is easier going for all, except the leader. During a migration, geese are apt to take turns in the lead position.

WORLD OF ANIMALS

■ We speak of a bale of turtles, a clowder of cats, a charm of goldfinches, a gam of whales, a knot of toads and a streak of tigers.

■ Some sharks swim in a figure eight when frightened.

■ Milk snakes lay about 13 eggs – in piles of animal manure.

■ Minnows have teeth in their throats.

■ The enormous livers of basking sharks, which can account for up to one-third of their body weight, produce a valuable oil used to lubricate engines and manufacture cosmetics.

■ Some species of freshwater eels migrate to the Sargasso Sea in the Atlantic Ocean to mate. After laying up to 20 million eggs, the female eel dies. The baby eels hatched from the eggs then make their way back to fresh water.

WORLD OF ANIMALS

■ More people are killed in Africa by crocodiles than by lions.

■ Some mantis shrimp travel by doing backward somersaults.

■ More species of fish live in a single tributary of the Amazon River than in all the rivers in North America combined.

■ More than two million southern fur seals – 95 per cent of the world's population – crowd onto the shores of South Georgia Island each summer. Half the world's population of southern elephant seals also come to the island to mate.

■ The European eagle owl is the largest owl in the world. It can measure 28 inches (70 centimetres) tall with a wingspan of five feet (150 centimetres) wide.

WORLD OF ANIMALS

■ The Everglades kite bird, in Florida, will only eat apple snails. The kites are becoming rare because as the Everglades dry up, the apple snails are dying out.

■ The eyes and nose of a frog are on top of its head, enabling it to breathe and see when most of its body is under the water.

■ Some species of rain forest birds migrate every summer from South America to Canada to breed.

■ The eyes of some birds weigh more than their brain. Likewise, their bones weigh less than their feathers.

■ Some species of starfish have as many as 50 appendages.

■ South America's harpy eagles eat monkeys. The birds build twig platforms in the treetops where they lay their eggs.

WORLD OF ANIMALS

■ Spider silk is an extremely strong material and its on-weight basis has been proven to be stronger than steel. Experts suggest that a pencil-thick strand of silk could stop a Boeing 747 in flight.

■ The fastest bird in the world is the Asian spine-tailed swift. In a level flight, it can reach a speed of 102 miles per hour (170 kilometres per hour).

■ Squirrels can climb trees faster than they can run on the ground.

■ The humpback whale's flippers grow to a maximum of 31 per cent of its body length – that's a potential maximum length of about 18 feet (5.5m). Because of these enormous flippers, the whale's Latin name translates to 'big-winged New Englander'.

■ The fastest dog, the greyhound, can reach speeds of up to 45 miles per hour. The breed was known to exist in ancient Egypt more than 5,000 years ago.

WORLD OF ANIMALS

■ Squirrels may live 15 or 20 years in captivity, but their life span in the wild is only about one year. They fall prey to disease, malnutrition, predators, cars and humans.

■ Starbuck, a Canadian bull who sired 200,000 dairy cows and an equal number of bulls in his life, earned an estimated $25 million before he died in 1998. After his death, his frozen semen was still selling for $250 a dose.

■ The female American oyster lays an average of 500 million eggs per year. Usually only one oyster out of the bunch reaches maturity.

■ Starfish feed on molluscs and crustaceans. In some areas, they are a serious threat to oyster and clam beds.

■ The jackrabbit is not a rabbit; it is a hare.

WORLD OF ANIMALS

■ Starfish have eyespots at the tip of each arm. These act as light sensors, and contain a red pigment which changes chemically in the presence of light. They are believed to influence the starfish's behaviour, particularly movement.

■ The kangaroo and the emu are the two animals found on the Australian coat of arms.

■ The killer whale, or orca, is the fastest sea mammal. It can reach speeds up to 34 miles per hour (56 kilometres per hour) in pursuit of prey.

■ The female anglerfish is six times larger than her mate. The male anchors himself to the top of her head and stays there for the rest of his life. They literally become one. Their digestive and circulatory systems are merged. Except for two very large generative organs and a few fins, nothing remains of the male.

WORLD OF ANIMALS

■ The killer whale, or orca, is not a whale but the largest member of the dolphin family.

■ The female blue crab can lay up to one million eggs in a day.

■ The female condor lays a single egg once every two years.

■ Jellyfish are comprised of more than 95 per cent water and have no brain, heart or bones, and no actual eyes.

■ The female green turtle sheds tears as she lays her eggs on the beach. This washes sand particles out of her eyes and rids her body of excess salt.

■ Studies show that the breeds of dogs that bite the least are, in order: the Golden Retriever, Labrador Retriever, Shetland Sheepdog, Old English Sheepdog and the Welsh Terrier.

WORLD OF ANIMALS

The female king crab incubates as many as 400,000 young for 11 months in a brood pouch under her abdomen.

Sue, the world's largest, most complete, and best preserved Tyrannosaurus Rex, made her grand debut to the public on 17 May 2000, at the Field Museum in Chicago, Illinois.

■ The female knot-tying weaverbird will refuse to mate with a male who has built a shoddy nest. If spurned, the male must take the nest apart and completely rebuild it in order to win the affections of the female.

■ Coral are closely related to jellyfish.

The female meadow vole can start reproducing when she is only 25 days old and gives birth to 16 litters per year.

Surviving all dangers, a wild cobra may live up to 20 years.

WORLD OF ANIMALS

■ The kinkajou's tail is twice as long as its body. Every night, it wraps itself up in its tail and uses it as a pillow.

■ The female pigeon cannot lay eggs if she is alone. In order for her ovaries to function, she must be able to see another pigeon. If no other pigeon is available, her own reflection in a mirror will suffice.

■ Tarantulas that are seen wandering around in the wild do not make good pets. These are sexually mature males at the end of their life cycle – they will die within a few weeks or months.

■ The kiwi, national bird of New Zealand, can't fly. It lives in a hole in the ground, is almost blind and lays only one egg each year. Despite this, it has survived for more than 70 million years.

WORLD OF ANIMALS

■ The female salamander inseminates herself. At mating time, the male deposits a conical mass of a jellylike substance containing the sperm. The female draws the jelly into herself, and in so doing, fertilizes her eggs.

■ The fennec fox is the smallest wild dog alive today. At birth the fennec weighs two pounds (0.8 kilograms) and will weigh three pounds (1.5 kilograms) in adulthood.

■ Terrier is from the Latin word 'terra' meaning 'earth'.

■ The koala is one of the few land animals that does not need to drink water to survive.

■ The two best known cat noises are roaring and purring. Only four species can roar, and they don't purr: lions, leopards, tigers and jaguars.

WORLD OF ANIMALS

■ The Kodiak grizzly bear is the world's largest meat-eating animal living on land. The Kodiak can weigh up to 500 pounds more than any other kind of bear.

■ The 20 million Mexican free-tail bats from Bracken Cave, Texas, eat approximately 200 tons of insects nightly.

■ The large hind feet of the chinchilla help it hop like a kangaroo, and its small front legs and feet are similar to those of a squirrel.

■ The largest bird egg in the world today is that of the ostrich. Ostrich eggs are from six to eight inches long. Because of their size and the thickness of their shells, they take 40 minutes to hard-boil.

■ The largest great white shark ever caught measured 37 feet and weighed 24,000 pounds. It was found in a herring weir in New Brunswick in 1930.

WORLD OF ANIMALS

The harmless whale shark holds the title of largest fish, with the record being a 59-footer captured in Thailand in 1919.

The first dinosaur appeared around 225 or 230 million years ago. It was called the Staurikosaurus and it survived for about five million years.

The first dinosaur to be found and recognized as a huge reptile was the Megalosaurus. This dinosaur was a meat eater.

The aardvark has such a well-developed sense of hearing, it can detect and locate distant ants on a nighttime march.

The first dinosaur to be given a name was the Iguanodon, found in Sussex, United Kingdom, in 1823. It was not the first dinosaur to be found.

The Adélie penguin bears the name of French explorer Dumont d'Urville's beloved wife.

WORLD OF ANIMALS

■ The first drawing of a North American swallowtail was of a male tiger swallowtail. It was drawn in 1587 by John White, commander of Sir Walter Raleigh's third expedition to North America.

■ The adjective 'murine' pertains to murids, the family of rodents that includes rats and mice.

■ The African eagle, swooping at more than 100 miles per hour, can brake to a halt in 20 feet.

■ The first flying animals were the pterosaurs that appeared over 200 million years ago. They were closer to flying reptiles than birds.

■ The first Komodo dragons to breed in the western world are at the National Zoo at the Smithsonian Institute in Washington, DC.

WORLD OF ANIMALS

■ The African lungfish can live without water for up to four years. When a drought occurs, it digs a pit and encloses itself in a capsule of slime and earth, leaving a small opening for breathing. The capsule dries and hardens, but the fish is protected. When rain comes, the capsule dissolves and the lungfish swims away.

■ The largest known egg ever laid by a creature was that of the extinct Aepyornis of Madagascar. The egg was 9.5 inches long. It had a volume of 2.35 gallons.

■ The first medical use of leeches dates back to approximately 2,500 years ago. The leech's saliva contains a property that acts as an anticoagulant for human blood.

■ The Alaskan moose is the largest deer of the New World. It attains a height at the withers in excess of seven feet and, when fully grown, weighs up to 1,800 pounds.

WORLD OF ANIMALS

The largest order of mammals, with about 1,700 species, is rodents. Bats are second with about 950 species.

The five fastest birds are: the peregrine falcon that can fly up to 175mph hour, the spine-tailed swift that can go 106mph, the frigate bird at 95mph, the spur-winged goose at 88mph, and the red-breasted merganser at 80mph.

■ The albatross can glide on air currents for several days and can even sleep while in flight.

■ The largest species of seahorse measures eight inches.

The albatross drinks sea water. It has a special desalinization apparatus that strains out and excretes all excess salt.

The last wolf in Great Britain was killed in Scotland, in 1743. Wolves were extinct in England by 1500.

WORLD OF ANIMALS

The leather coral, which is softer than the stony corals, may attack and eat one of its own kind if subjected to crowded conditions.

The leech has 32 brains.

The leech will gorge itself up to five times its body weight and then just fall off its victim.

The flounder swims sideways.

The flying fish builds up speed in the water then leaps into the air to escape predators. Once in the air, it can stay airborne for up to 325 feet (100m).

The flying snake of Java and Malaysia is able to flatten itself out like a ribbon and sail like a glider from tree to tree.

The American opossum, a marsupial, bears its young just 12 to 13 days after conception.

WORLD OF ANIMALS

■ The Asiatic elephant takes 608 days to give birth, or just over 20 months.

■ The fur of the vicuna, a small member of the camel family which lives in the Andes mountains of Peru, is so fine that each hair is less than two-thousandths of an inch. The animal was considered sacred by the Incas, and only royalty could wear its fleece.

■ The American woodcock, with its eyes placed towards the top of its head, can see backward and upward, and forward and upward, with binocular vision and, laterally, almost 180 degrees with each eye.

■ The gait of the giraffe is a pace, with both legs on one side moving together. Because of its long stride, a giraffe is quicker than it appears. The animal, at full gallop, can run about 30 miles per hour.

WORLD OF ANIMALS

■ The anaconda, one of the world's largest snakes, gives birth to its young instead of laying eggs.

■ The lethal Lion's Mane jellyfish has a bell reaching up to eight feet in diameter, and tentacles longer than a blue whale – up to 200 feet long. Juveniles are pink, turning red as they mature, and then becoming brownish purple when adults.

■ The garfish has green bones.

■ The ancient nautilus is considered the most intelligent of the invertebrates; it is said to have been as intelligent as a young cat.

■ The life expectancy of the average mockingbird is 10 years.

■ The gastric juices of a snake can digest bones and teeth – but not fur or hair.

■ The anteater hasn't any teeth or jaws. Its sticky tongue measures over a foot long.

WORLD OF ANIMALS

■ The longest fish is the oarfish, which is shaped like an eel. On average, it grows to over 20 feet (six metres) in length, but oarfish of 46 feet (14 metres) have been found.

■ The gecko lizard can run on the ceiling without falling because its toes have flaps of skin that act like suction cups.

■ The antlers of a male moose can have as many as 30 tines, or spikes.

■ The longest lizard in the world is the Komodo dragon at 10 feet long. Next are the water monitor at 8.8 feet, then the perenty at 7.8 feet, the common iguana at five feet and the marine iguana at five feet.

■ The gestation period for giraffes is about 14 to 15 months.

WORLD OF ANIMALS

■ The antlers of a moose are created from living tissue supplied by blood through a network of vessels covered with a soft smooth skin called velvet. Eventually the tissue becomes solidified, the velvet is scraped off, and the antlers become completely formed of dead matter.

■ The loudest bird in the world is the male bellbird, found in Central and South America. To attract mates, the male makes a clanging sound like a bell that can be heard from miles away.

■ The armour of the armadillo is not as tough as it appears. It is very pliable, much like a human fingernail.

■ The male argus pheasant of Asia has the longest feathers of all the flying birds. Its tails feathers can reach a length of six feet (1.7 metres).

■ The male fox will mate for life and, if the female dies, he remains single for the rest of his life. However, if the male dies, the female will hook up with a new mate.

WORLD OF ANIMALS

■ The male house wren builds several nests as part of his courtship ritual. Once the nests are completed, his potential bride looks them all over, then selects one as her preferred choice for the laying of her eggs.

■ The male moose sheds its antlers every winter and grows a new set the following year.

■ The giant African snail grows to a foot long and reaches weights greater than a pound.

■ The giant armadillo has as many as 100 teeth, although they are small and fragile.

■ The giant flying foxes that live in Indonesia have wingspans of nearly six feet.

■ The giant Pacific octopus can fit its entire body through an opening no bigger than the size of its beak.

WORLD OF ANIMALS

There are close to one million sheep in Iceland.

The giant squid is the largest creature without a backbone. It weighs up to 2.5 tons and grows up to 55 feet long. Each eye is a foot or more in diameter.

There are eleven species of hedgehog native to Africa, Asia and Europe.

The Gila monster spends about 96 per cent of its life underground.

There are fewer than 1,000 Bactrian camels left in the wild. They have survived in a land with no water in an area used for nuclear testing. Their numbers, however, are falling dramatically as humans encroach farther and farther into China's Gobi Desert.

The male seahorse, not the female, carries the embryo of the species. The female fills the male's brooch pouch with eggs, which remain in the swollen sac for a gestation period of eight to ten days.

WORLD OF ANIMALS

■ The giraffe's heart is huge; it weighs 25 pounds, is two feet long and has walls up to three inches thick.

■ There are fewer than 1,000 giant pandas left alive in the world.

■ The massive skeleton of the African elephant accounts for about 15 per cent of the body weight, just as in a man of slender build; however, the elephant's skeleton supports as much as four tons per leg, and is thus stressed close to the physical limit for bone. To keep from damaging its skeleton, an African elephant has to move sedately, never jumping or running. The 'charge' of these animals is a fast walk on long legs, at about 15 miles per hour.

■ The girth of the Gila monster lizard's tail may shrink by 80 per cent during times of low food supply.

■ There are lavender, grey and blond skunks.

WORLD OF ANIMALS

■ The glue of a barnacle cannot be dissolved with strong acids or temperatures set as high as 440°F.

■ There are mice that nest in trees. These creatures may spend their whole life without ever touching the ground.

■ The minuscule krill shrimp has eleven pairs of legs.

■ There are more caribou in Alaska than people.

■ There are more goats than cows in mountainous countries since goats can survive well by eating grass and other brush.

■ The Mola Mola, or Ocean Sunfish, lays up to 5 million eggs at one time.

WORLD OF ANIMALS

■ The more that is learned about the ecological benefits of bats, the more home gardeners are going out of their way to entice these amazing winged mammals into their neighbourhoods. Bats are voracious insect eaters, devouring as many as 600 bugs per hour for four to six hours a night. They can eat from one-half to three-quarters their weight per evening. Bats are also important plant pollinators, particularly in the southwestern United States.

■ There are more species of fish than mammals, reptiles and birds combined.

■ The most carnivorous of all bears is the polar bear. Its diet consists almost entirely of seals and fish.

■ The most venomous of all snakes, the Inland Taipan, has enough venom in one bite to kill more than 200,000 mice.

■ The mouse is the most common mammal in the United States.

WORLD OF ANIMALS

The grey whale is not really grey. It is black and just appears grey from a distance.

The grey whale, a baleen whale, has a series of up to 180 fringed overlapping plates hanging from each side of its upper jaw. This is where teeth would be located if the creature had any.

■ The grey wolf is the largest wild dog alive today. As an adult a grey wolf can weigh up to 176 pounds (80 kilograms).

■ There are more than 100 million dogs and cats in the United States.

Americans spend more than 5.4 billion dollars on their pets each year.

The great distance between the eyes and nostrils of the hammerhead shark may allow the animal to detect its prey's direction more accurately. They are experts at catching the stingrays on which they feed.

WORLD OF ANIMALS

■ There are more than 150 breeds of horses in the world.

■ With nearly 11 million horses within its borders, China is the leader of all nations for horse population.

■ The great horned owl can turn its head 270 degrees.

■ There are more than 450 species of finches throughout the world.

■ The mudskipper is a fish that can actually walk on land.

■ The grebe, an aquatic bird, has an effective means of escaping danger while protecting its young. At the first sign of danger, it will sink into the water until its back is level with the surface. This allows its offspring to swim over and quickly climb on to its back. The parent grebe then rises up to its swimming position and ferries the chicks across the water to safety.

WORLD OF ANIMALS

■ There are no penguins at the North Pole. In fact, there are no penguins anywhere in the Northern Hemisphere (outside of zoos). All 17 varieties of the bird are found below the equator, primarily in Antarctica.

■ The musk ox has the longest hair of any polar animal. The hairs of the outer layer of their coats can reach up to three feet (one metre) long.

■ There are over 300 species of parrots.

■ The grizzly bear is capable of running as fast as the average horse.

■ There are no wild deer of any kind in Australia, and the small red deer is the only one found in Africa.

■ The nearly 1,000 kinds of bats account for almost a quarter of all mammal species, and most are highly beneficial.

WORLD OF ANIMALS

■ The groundhog is a member of the rodent family. The typical adult groundhog can weigh approximately eight to 14 pounds and average about 22 inches in length.

■ The nematode Caenorhabditis elegans ages the equivalent of five human years for every day they live, usually expiring after 14 days. However, when stressed, the worm goes into a state of suspended animation that can last for two months or more. The human equivalent would be to sleep for about 200 years.

■ The gurnard, a fish found in Florida, grunts when a thunderstorm is brewing, and it's said to be more reliable than meteorologists.

■ There are seven distinctive types of combs on chickens: rose, strawberry, single, cushion, buttercup, pea and V-shaped.

WORLD OF ANIMALS

■ The nest of the African Grey Parrot is a hole in a large tree. The bird uses no nesting material. It lays its eggs in the wood dust at the bottom of the nest-holes, which are about two to six feet deep (60 to 200cm).

■ There are seven species of bears: the American black bear, the Asian black bear, the brown bear, the polar bear, the sloth bear, the spectacled bear and the sun bear.

■ The nest of the bald eagle can weigh well over a ton.

■ There are some 50 different species of sea snakes, and all of them are venomous. They thrive in abundance along the coast from the Persian Gulf to Japan and around Australia and Melanesia. Their venom is 10 times as virulent as that of the cobra. Humans bitten by them have died within two-and-a-half hours.

WORLD OF ANIMALS

■ The New Guinea singing dog's most unique characteristic is its dramatic ability to vary the pitch of its howl. The animal does not bark repetitively but has a complex vocal behaviour, including yelps, whines and single-note howls.

■ There are species of mice that live in marshy places and are excellent swimmers.

■ The Nile crocodile averages about 45 years in the wild, and may live up to 80 years in captivity.

■ The normal body temperature of the Clydesdale horse is 101°F (38°C).

■ The hare can travel up to 45 miles per hour, whereas the rabbit can achieve an average speed of just 35 miles per hour.

■ The heaviest bird in the world is the Kori bustard. The Kori weighs around 31 pounds (14 kilograms) on average, but the largest one found was over 40 pounds (18 kilograms).

WORLD OF ANIMALS

■ The heaviest flighted birds in the world are the great bustard at 40 pounds, the trumpeter swan at 37 pounds, the mute swan at 36 pounds, the albatross at 34 pounds and the whooper swan at 34 pounds.

■ There is a strong bond between mother and child among orangutans. Orangutan infants cling almost continually to their mothers until they are one years old.

■ The hides of mature female blue sharks are more than twice as thick as those of males, probably as a protection against courtship bites.

■ The hippopotamus gives birth under water and nurses its young in the river as well, although the young hippos must come up periodically for air.

■ There is just one known species of ostrich in the world – it is in the order of Struthioniformes.

WORLD OF ANIMALS

■ The now-extinct ancestor of the horse, eohippus, had a short neck, a pug muzzle and stood no higher than a medium-sized dog.

■ The hippopotamus has skin an inch-and-a-half thick; it's so solid that most bullets cannot penetrate it.

■ There is no mention of cats or rats in the Bible.

■ The nurse shark spends much of its time in caves. It leaves the security of its cave to feed on prey such as lobsters, squid and crabs. The sucking sound of its powerful throat muscles is probably the origin of the animal's common name.

■ The hippopotamus has the world's shortest sperm.

■ There is no single cat called the panther. The name is commonly applied to the leopard, but it is also used to refer to the puma and the jaguar. A black panther is really a black leopard.

WORLD OF ANIMALS

■ The odour of a skunk can be detected by a human a mile away.

■ The hippopotamus is, next to the elephant, the heaviest of all land mammals. It may weigh as much as 8,000 pounds. It is also a close relative of the pig.

■ There once were more sea lions on earth than people.

■ The once popular dog name 'Fido' is from Latin and means 'fidelity'.

■ The Hirudo leech has three jaws with 100 teeth on each jaw – making 300 teeth in all.

■ The Amazon leech uses a different method of sucking blood. They insert a long proboscis into the victim as opposed to biting.

WORLD OF ANIMALS

■ There were two main types of dinosaurs. Saurischia dinosaurs had hip and pelvic bones like lizards and consisted of meat – and plant – eating dinosaurs. Ornithischia dinosaurs had hip and pelvic bones like birds and consisted of small plant-eaters.

■ The only country in the world that has a Bill of Rights for cows is India.

■ There were about 60 million bison when the Europeans landed in America. By the 1880s, all but 500 bison were killed. Today there are 350,000 bison in America.

■ The only dog to ever appear in a Shakespearean play was Crab in *The Two Gentlemen of Verona*.

■ Thinking that a giraffe's parents were a camel and a leopard, the Europeans once called the animal a 'camelopard'.

WORLD OF ANIMALS

■ The only two mammals to lay eggs are the platypus and the echidna. The mothers nurse their babies through pores in their skin.

■ Thirty thousand monkeys were used in the massive three-year effort to classify the various types of polio.

■ The onomatopoeia for a dog's bark in Japanese is wan-wan.

■ The opossum, often called 'possum', dates back over 45 million years.

■ The optimum depth of water in a birdbath is two-and-a-half inches. Less water makes it difficult for birds to take a bath; more makes them afraid.

■ The Hirudo leech lays its babies within a cocoon; the Amazon leech carries its babies on its stomach – sometimes as many as 300.

WORLD OF ANIMALS

■ The Honduran white bat is snow white with a yellow nose and ears. It cuts large leaves to make 'tents' that protect its small colonies from jungle rains.

■ The horned lizard of the American southwest may squirt a thin stream of blood from the corners of its eyes when frightened.

■ The horned owl is not horned. Two tufts of feathers were mistaken for horns.

■ Thoroughbred horses are so thin-skinned their veins are visible beneath the skin, especially on the legs.

■ The horns of a bighorn sheep can weigh 40 pounds.

■ Though human noses have an impressive five million olfactory cells with which to smell, sheepdogs have 220 million, enabling them to smell 44 times better than man.

WORLD OF ANIMALS

■ Though small, the Shetland pony is strong. It was once used to haul heavy cars in coal-mines.

■ The ostrich has four eyelids. The inner lids are for blinking and keeping the eyeballs moist, the outer lids for casting come-hither glances at potential mates.

■ The howler monkey is the loudest animal living in the rainforests of South America. Their voices can be heard up to five miles (eight kilometres) away.

■ Though the Connecticut warbler passes through Connecticut only on its autumn migration, this shy, seldom-seen songbird bears the name of the state where it was first collected by pioneer ornithologist Alexander Wilson in 1812.

■ The ostrich has only two toes, unlike most birds, which have three or four.

WORLD OF ANIMALS

■ The hum of a hummingbird comes from the super-fast beat of the wings. The smallest ones beat their wings the fastest – up to 80 times per second. Even the slower beat of bigger hummingbirds' wings (20 times per second) is so fast you can only see a blur.

■ Tiger cubs are born blind and weigh only about two to three pounds (1kg), depending on the subspecies. They live on milk for six to eight weeks before the female begins taking them to kills to feed. Tigers have fully developed canines by 16 months of age, but they do not begin making their own kills until about 18 months of age.

■ The owl is the only bird to drop its upper eyelid to wink. All other birds raise their lower eyelids.

■ The hummingbird is the only bird that can fly backwards.

WORLD OF ANIMALS

■ Tigers have stripes to help them hide in the rainforest undergrowth. The black and gold stripes break up the outline of the tiger's body making it very hard to see.

■ The owl parrot can't fly, and builds its nest under tree roots.

■ The hummingbird's tiny brain, 4.2 per cent of its body weight, is proportionately the largest in the bird kingdom.

■ Time and erosion have erased 99 per cent of all dinosaur footprints.

■ The oyster is usually ambisexual. It begins life as a male, then becomes a female, then changes back to being a male, then back to being female. It may go back and forth many times.

■ Tiny woolly bats, in West Africa, live in the large webs of colonial spiders.

WORLD OF ANIMALS

■ The Ozark blind salamander begins life with eyes and plumelike gills. As the animal matures, its eyelids fuse together and the gills disappear.

■ To a human, one giant octopus looks virtually the same as any other of the same size and species. This explains why divers claim to have seen the same octopus occupy a den for ten or more years. But an octopus seldom lives longer than four years.

■ The pair of fins at the back of a fish's body are called pelvic fins.

■ To be called a mammal, the female must feed her young on milk she has produced.

■ The pallid bat of western North America is immune to the stings of scorpions, as well as the seven-inch centipedes upon which it feeds.

WORLD OF ANIMALS

The part of the foot of a horse between the fetlock and the hoof is the pastern.

The pelican breathes through its mouth because it has no nostrils.

To keep from being separated while sleeping, sea otters tie themselves together with kelp, often drifting miles out to sea during the night.

To safeguard its food when away, the wolverine marks it with a strong musk so foul smelling that other animals won't touch it.

The penculine titmouse of Africa builds its home in such a sturdy manner that Masai tribesman use their nests for purses and carrying cases.

To survive, most birds must eat at least half their own weight in food each day.

The penguin is the only bird that can swim, but not fly. It is also the only bird that walks upright.

WORLD OF ANIMALS

To warn off other males, the orangutans of South-east Asia burp loudly to declare their territory.

The pichiciego is a little-known burrowing South American animal that is related to the armadillo, but is smaller in size. The ending of the animal's name is derived from the Spanish *ciego*, meaning 'blind.'

■ Toads eat only moving prey.

■ The pigmy shrew – a relative of the mole – is the smallest mammal in North America. It weighs $1/14$ ounce – less than a 5p piece.

Today's oldest form of horse is the Przewalski, or Mongolian Wild Horse. Survivors of this breed were discovered in the Gobi Desert in 1881.

The pistol shrimp makes a noise so loud that it can shatter glass.

WORLD OF ANIMALS

■ Travelling at a rate of two to three miles per hour, camels can carry 500 to 1,000 pounds on their backs. They are able to keep up this pace for six or seven hours a day. Camels will refuse to carry loads that are not properly balanced.

■ The pitohui bird of Papua New Guinea has enough poison in its feathers and skin to kill mice and frogs. The poison can affect humans, often causing them numbness, burning and snoozing.

■ Tree frogs can climb windowpanes.

■ The polar bear is the only bear that has hair on the soles of its feet. This protects the animal's feet from the cold and prevents slipping on the ice.

■ Tuna swim at a steady rate of nine miles per hour for an indefinite period of time – and they never stop moving. Estimates indicate that a 15-year-old tuna travels one million miles in its lifetime.

WORLD OF ANIMALS

■ Tunas will suffocate if they ever stop swimming. They need a continual flow of water across their gills to breathe, even while they rest.

■ The porcupine's love for salt often leads the animal to roadways or walkways where salt has been sprinkled to melt the ice. They will lick and gnaw on anything containing salt, such as saddles, canoe paddles and axe handles.

■ Turtles survived the upheavals of the last 200 million years, including the great extinction episode that eliminated the dinosaurs. Now, about half of the world's turtle species face possible extinction – due in large part to a growing demand for turtles as a popular dining delicacy and a source of traditional medicines.

WORLD OF ANIMALS

■ The Portuguese man-of-war is found most commonly in the Gulf Stream of the northern Atlantic Ocean and in the tropical and subtropical regions of the Indian and Pacific Oceans. It is sometimes found floating in groups numbering in the thousands.

■ Turtles, tortoises and terrapins do not have teeth. They have hard, horny jaws that are able to cut and tear food.

■ The prescribed diet of the Polish Lowland Sheepdog in present-day Poland consists of bread, potatoes, cottage cheese, milk and an occasional egg.

■ Two rats can become the progenitors of 15,000 rats in less than a year.

■ The pronghorn antelope can run at up to 61 miles per hour.

■ Unlike most female animals, the female rice rat is the one that searches for and pursues a mate.

WORLD OF ANIMALS

■ Unlike most fish, electric eels cannot get enough oxygen from water. Approximately every five minutes, they must surface to breathe or they will drown. Unlike most fish, they can swim both backwards and forwards.

■ Unlike most other large cats, snow leopards cannot roar.

■ The quahog, a marine clam, can live for up to 200 years, making it the longest living ocean creature in the world. Second place goes to the killer whale at 90 years; third is the blue whale at 80 years; fourth is the sea turtle at 50 years, and fifth is the tiger shark at 40 years.

■ The racoon derives its name from the Indian word meaning 'he who scratches with his hands'.

WORLD OF ANIMALS

■ The rare Hawaiian monk seal has been known to dive to about 1,650 feet (500m). The animal doesn't 'bark' like sea lions, but has a number of different vocalizations that it produces, including a deep, guttural call that sounds much like a belch.

■ Unlike other reptiles, female alligators protect their young for up to two years after hatching.

■ The acorn woodpecker leaves its food sticking out of the holes it's drilled in oak trees, making it easy for squirrels and jays to help themselves.

■ Unrelated to the chicken, the male cock-of-the-rock bird earned the name 'cock' because of its rooster-like appearance and combative behaviour. The female of the species influenced the word 'rock' being added to the name because of her habit of nesting and rearing the young in sheltered rock niches.

WORLD OF ANIMALS

■ Until he's about 21 years old, the male Indian elephant isn't interested in romancing a female elephant.

■ Until they were imported into the country, Australia did not have any members of the cat family, hoofed animals, apes or monkeys.

■ Using its web – the skin between its arms – an octopus can carry up to a dozen crabs back to its den.

■ Vampire bats adopt orphans and have been known to risk their lives to share food with less fortunate roost-mates.

■ Vampire bats don't suck blood; they drink it. By making small cuts in the skin of a sleeping animal, while their saliva numbs the area, the bat laps up the blood.

■ Vampire bats need about two tablespoonfuls of blood each day. The creature is able to extract its dinner in approximately 20 minutes.

WORLD OF ANIMALS

■ Very unusually for carnivores, hyena clans are dominated by females.

■ Victorian society rejected the notion that pets were capable of feelings or expressing emotion.

■ Walking catfish of Florida can stay out of water for 80 days.

■ Wandering albatross devote a full year to raising their babies.

THAT'S ENTERTAINMENT

THAT'S ENTERTAINMENT

An anchor is tattooed on Popeye's arm.

After the Popeye strip started in 1931, spinach consumption went up by 33 per cent in the US.

Before Mickey Mouse, Felix the Cat was the most popular cartoon character.

Bill Cosby created Fat Albert and Weird Harold.

Bugs Bunny first said, 'What's up, doc?' in the 1940 cartoon 'A Wild Hare.'

Casey Kasem is the voice of Shaggy on *Scooby-Doo*.

Charlie Brown's father was a barber.

Cheryl Ladd (of *Charlie's Angels* fame) played the voice, both talking and singing, of Josie in the 70s Saturday morning cartoon *Josie and the Pussycats*.

THAT'S ENTERTAINMENT

Cinderella's real name is Ella.

Daisy is the name of Dagwood Bumstead's dog.

Beetle from the comic strip 'Beetle Bailey' and Lois from the comic strip 'Hi and Lois' are brother and sister.

Goofy actually started life as 'Dippy Dawg', a combination of both Goofy and Pluto.

Donald Duck comics were banned in Finland because he doesn't wear pants.

Donald Duck's middle name is Fauntleroy.

Donald Duck's sister is called Dumbella.

Elzie Crisler Segar created the comic strip character Popeye in 1919.

THAT'S ENTERTAINMENT

■ Felix the Cat is the first cartoon character to ever have been made into a balloon for a parade.

■ Goofy had a wife, Mrs Goofy and one son, Goofy Jr.

■ In an episode of *The Simpsons*, Sideshow Bob's Criminal Number is 24601, the same as the Criminal number of Jean Valjean in *Les Miserables*.

■ Kathleen Turner was the voice of Jessica Rabbit, and Amy Irving was her singing voice.

■ Lucy and Linus (who were brother and sister) had another little brother named Rerun. (He sometimes played left-field on Charlie Brown's baseball team, when he could find it!).

■ Marmaduke (the cartoon dog) is a great dane.

THAT'S ENTERTAINMENT

■ Matt Groening, creator of *The Simpsons*, incorporated his initials into the drawing of Homer. M is his hair and G is his ear.

■ Mickey Mouse is known as 'Topolino' in Italy. He was the first non-human to win an Oscar.

■ Mickey Mouse's ears are always turned to the front, no matter which direction his head is pointing.

■ 18 November is Mickey Mouse's birthday.

■ Of the four Teenage Mutant Ninja Turtles, all named after artists and/or sculptors, Donatello does not occur in the same time period as Leonardo, Michelangelo and Raphael.

■ On *Scooby Doo*, Shaggy's real name is Norville.

THAT'S ENTERTAINMENT

On the cartoon show *The Jetsons*, Jane is 33 years old and her daughter Judy is 18.

Peanuts is the world's most read comic strip.

Photographer Peter Parker's secret identity is Spiderman.

Pokemon stands for pocket monster.

Popeye was five feet, six inches tall.

Rocky Racoon lives in the Black Hills of South Dakota.

Scooby Doo's first real name is Scoobert.

Superman's boyhood home was Smallville, Illinois.

The Black Cauldron is the only PG-rated Disney animated feature.

The Flintstones live at 39 Stone Canyon Way, Bedrock.

THAT'S ENTERTAINMENT

The Looney Tunes song is actually called 'the merry-go-round is broken down'.

The most common set of initials for Superman's friends and enemies is LL.

The movie playing at the drive-in at the beginning of *The Flintstones* was *The Monster*.

The name of Dennis the Menace's dog is Gnasher.

The name of Popeye's adopted son is Swee'pea.

The Simpsons is the longest running animated series on TV.

The voice of Tony the Tiger is Thurl Ravenscroft.

Tweety used to be a baby bird without feathers until the censors made him have feathers because he looked naked.

THAT'S ENTERTAINMENT

Walt Disney named Mickey Mouse after Mickey Rooney, whose mother he dated for some time.

Walt Disney originally supplied the voice for his character Mickey Mouse.

Wilma Flintstone's maiden name was Wilma Slaghoopal, and Betty Rubble's was Betty Jean Mcbricker.

Yasser Arafat is addicted to watching television cartoons.

According to Pope Innocent III, it was not a crime to kill someone after a game of chess.

Australia is considered the easiest continent to defend in the game 'Risk.'

Mario, of Super Mario Bros. fame, appeared in the 1981 arcade game Donkey Kong. His original name was Jumpman, but was changed to Mario to honour the Nintendo of America's landlord, Mario Segali.

THAT'S ENTERTAINMENT

Parker Brothers prints about 50 billion dollars' worth of Monopoly money in one year.

Since its introduction in February 1935, more than 150 million Monopoly board games have been sold worldwide.

Since the Lego Group began manufacturing blocks in 1949, more than 189 billion pieces in 2000 different shapes have been produced. This is enough for about 30 Lego pieces for every living person on earth.

The colour black moves first in draughts.

The longest Monopoly game in a bathtub was 99 hours long.

The Ouija board is named after the French and German words for yes – *oui* and *ja*.

The total number of bridge hands possible is 54 octillion.

THAT'S ENTERTAINMENT

The word checkmate in chess comes from the Persian phrase *Shah-Mat* which means 'the king is dead'.

There are 100 squares on a 'Snakes and Ladders' board.

There are 311,875,200 five-card hands possible in a 52-card deck of cards.

There are 225 spaces on a Scrabble board.

Trivial Pursuit was invented by Canadians Scott Abbott and Chris Haney. They didn't want to pay the £10.50 price for Scrabble, so they made up their own game.

Values on the Monopoly gameboard are the same today as they were in 1935.

Westwood Studios' computer game 'Command and Conquer' is the most successful war game series of all time according to the *Guinness Book of World Records*.

THAT'S ENTERTAINMENT

101 Dalmatians and *Peter Pan* are the only two Disney cartoon features with both parents that are present and don't die throughout the movie.

A walla-walla scene is one where extras pretend to be talking in the back-ground – when they say walla-walla it looks like they are actually talking.

All of the clocks in the movie *Pulp Fiction* are stuck on 4:20.

Bruce was the nickname of the mechanical shark used in the *Jaws* movies.

C3PO is the first character to speak in *Star Wars*.

Cleopatra cost over £28 million to produce in 1963.

Darth Vader is the only officer in the Imperial Forces who doesn't have a rank.

Debra Winger was the voice of ET.

THAT'S ENTERTAINMENT

Dirty Harry's last name is Callahan.

During the chariot scene in *Ben Hur* a small red car can be seen in the distance.

Felix Leiter is James Bond's CIA contact.

Four people played Darth Vader: David Prowse was his body, James Earl Jones did the voice, Sebastian Shaw was his face and a fourth person did the breathing.

In Disney's *Fantasia*, the sorcerer's name is Yensid (Disney spelled backwards).

In *Psycho*, the colour of Mrs Bates's dress was periwinkle blue.

In the *Return of the Jedi* special edition during the new Couruscant footage at the end of the film a stormtrooper can be seen being carried over the crowds.

THAT'S ENTERTAINMENT

■ In the 1983 film *JAWS 3D* the shark blows up. Some of the shark guts were stuffed ET dolls being sold at the time.

■ In the early days of silent films, there was blatant thievery. Unscrupulous film companies would steal the film, reshoot a scene or two and release it as a new production. To combat this, the Biograph company put the company's trade mark initials AB somewhere in every scene – on a door, a wall, or window.

■ In the film '*Star Trek: First Contact*', when Picard shows Lilly she is orbiting earth, Australia and Papua New Guinea are clearly visible... but New Zealand is missing.

■ In the *Mario Brothers* movie, the Princess's first name is Daisy, but in Mario 64, the game, her first name is Peach. Before that, it's Princess Toadstool.

THAT'S ENTERTAINMENT

In the movie 'Now and Then', when the girls are talking to the hippie (Brendan Fraser) and they get up to leave, Teeny (Thora Birch) puts out her cigarette twice.

In The Wizard of Oz, Dorothy's last name is Gale.

James Bond is known as 'Mr Kiss-Kiss-Bang-Bang' in Italy.

James Bond likes his martinis shaken, not stirred.

Jean-Claude Van Damme was the alien in the original Predator in almost all the jumping and climbing scenes.

King Kong is the only movie to have its sequel (Son of Kong) released the same year (1933).

King Kong was Adolf Hitler's favourite movie.

THAT'S ENTERTAINMENT

■ *Love Me Tender* was Elvis Presley's first film.

■ Luke Skywalker's last name was changed at the last minute from Starkiller in order to make it less violent.

■ More bullets were fired in *Starship Troopers* than in any other movie made.

■ Mrs Claus's first name is Jessica in the movie *Santa Claus is Coming to Town*.

■ *Pulp Fiction* cost $8 million to make. $5 million went on actor's salaries.

■ Skull island is the jungle home of King Kong.

■ The 1st time the 'f-word' was spoken in a movie was by Marianne Faithfull in the 1968 film, *I'll Never Forget Whatshisname*. In Brian De Palma's 1984 movie, *Scarface*, the word is spoken 206 times – an average of once every 29 seconds.

THAT'S ENTERTAINMENT

■ The famous theme ostensibly from 'Dragnet' was actually composed by Miklos Rozsa for the 1946 film noir classic The Killers.

■ The first female monster to appear on the big screen was the Bride of Frankenstein.

■ The first James Bond movie was 'Dr No.'

■ The first real motion picture theatre was called a Nickelodeon (admission was a nickel) and opened in McKeesport Pennsylvania near Pittsburg. The first motion picture shown there was The Great Train Robbery.

■ The first word spoken by an ape in the movie Planet of the Apes was 'smile'.

■ The Lion King is the top grossing Disney movie of all-time with domestic gross intake of $312 million.

THAT'S ENTERTAINMENT

■ The longest film ever released was **** by Andy Warhol, which lasted 24 hours. It proved, not surprisingly (except perhaps to its creator), an utter failure. It was withdrawn and re-released in a 90-minute form as *The Loves of Ondine*.

■ The longest Hollywood kiss was from the 1941 film *You're in the Army Now*, it lasted three minutes and three seconds.

■ The mask used by Michael Myers in the original *Halloween* was actually a Captain Kirk mask painted white.

■ The movie *Cleopatra*, starring Elizabeth Taylor, was banned from Egypt in 1963 because she was a Jewish convert.

■ The movie *Braveheart* was filmed in Ireland.

■ The movie *Clue* has three different endings. Each ending was randomly chosen for different theatres. All three endings are present in the home video.

THAT'S ENTERTAINMENT

The movie *Paris, Texas* was banned in the city Paris, Texas shortly after its box office release.

The name for Oz in *The Wizard of Oz* was thought up when the creator, Frank Baum, looked at his filing cabinet and saw A–N and O–Z, hence Oz.

The name of Jabba the Hut's pet spider monkey is Salacious Crumb.

The name of the dog from *The Grinch Who Stole Christmas* was Max.

The number of the trash compactor in *Star Wars* is 3263827.

The second unit films movie shots that do not require the presence of actors.

The skyscraper in *Die Hard* is the Century Fox Tower.

The sound of ET walking was made by someone squishing her hands in jelly.

THAT'S ENTERTAINMENT

The word 'mafia' was purposely omitted from the *Godfather* screenplay.

When a film is in production, the last shot of the day is the martini shot, the next to last one is the Abby Singer.

When the movie *The Wizard of Oz* first came out, it got bad reviews. The critics said it was stupid and uncreative.

A violin actually contains 70 separate pieces of wood.

Abbey Road was the last album recorded by the Beatles.

Aerosmith's 'Dude looks like a lady,' was written about Vince Neil of Motley Crue.

Andy Warhol created the Rolling Stones' emblem depicting the big tongue. It first appeared on the cover of the *Sticky Fingers* album.

THAT'S ENTERTAINMENT

Beethoven's Fifth was the first symphony to include trombones.

Don MacLean's song 'American Pie' was written about Buddy Holly, The Big Bopper and Richie Valens. All three were on the same plane that crashed.

Glass flutes do not expand with humidity so their owners are spared the nuisance of tuning them.

'Happy Birthday To You' is the most often sung song in America.

In 1976, Rodrigo's 'Guitar Concierto de Aranjuez' was No 1 in the UK for only three hours because of a computer error.

20252 is Smokey the Bear's own zip code.

A Chinese chequerboard has 121 holes.

Alfred Hitchcock never won an Academy Award for directing.

THAT'S ENTERTAINMENT

Approximately 60 circus performers have been shot from cannons. At last report, 31 of these have been killed.

Because metal was scarce, the Oscars given out during World War II were made of wood.

Boris Karloff is the narrator of the seasonal television special *How the Grinch Stole Christmas*.

Breath, by Samuel Beckett, was first performed in April 1970. The play lasts thirty seconds, has no actors and no dialogue.

Bret Hart trademarked the nickname 'Hitman' in 1990.

Carnegie Mellon University offers bag piping as a major.

Dirty Harry's badge number is 2211.

THAT'S ENTERTAINMENT

Dracula is the most filmed story of all time *Dr Jekyll and Mr Hyde* is second and *Oliver Twist* is third.

Every day more money is printed for Monopoly than the US Treasury.

Godzilla has made the covers of *Time* and *Newsweek*.

Gone With the Wind is the only Civil War epic ever filmed without a single battle scene.

In 1938, Joe Shuster and Jerry Siegel sold all rights to the comic-strip character Superman to their publishers for $130.

In the game Monopoly, the most money you can lose in one travel around the board (normal game rules, going to jail only once) is $26,040. The most money you can lose in one turn is $5,070.

It is bad luck to say 'Macbeth' in a theatre.

THAT'S ENTERTAINMENT

Kermit the Frog has 11 points on his collar around his neck.

Kermit the Frog is left-handed.

Kermit the Frog was named after Kermit Scott, a childhood friend of Jim Henson's, who became a professor of philosophy at Purdue University.

Miss Piggy's measurements are 27-20-36.

Of the six men who made up the Three Stooges, three of them were real brothers (Moe, Curly and Shemp).

Ronald Reagan did a narration at the 1947 Oscar ceremony.

Sleeping Beauty slept 100 years.

The Simpsons live at 742 Evergreen Terrace, Springfield and The Munsters at 1313 Mockingbird Lane, Mockingbird Heights.

THAT'S ENTERTAINMENT

Steely Dan got their name from a sexual device depicted in the book *The Naked Lunch*.

Superman's name on Krypton was Kal-El.

The Academy Award statue is named after a librarian's uncle. One day Margaret Herrick, librarian for the Academy of Motion Picture Arts and Sciences, made the remark that the statue looked like her Uncle Oscar, and the name stuck.

The average British family views television six hours each day.

The first US discotheque was the Whiskey-A-Go-Go in LA.

The literal translation for *kung-fu* is leisure time.

The most common name in nursery rhymes is Jack.

THAT'S ENTERTAINMENT

■ The music hall entertainer Nosmo King derived his stage name from a 'No Smoking' sign.

■ The tango originated as a dance between two men (for partnering practice).

■ There are 22 stars surrounding the mountain on the Paramount Pictures logo.

■ There are Pokemon school books. You can even do maths with a Pokemon maths book.

■ In 1990, there were an estimated 75,000 accordionists in the United States.

■ In every show that Tom Jones and Harvey Schmidt (The Fantasticks) did there was at least one song about rain.

THAT'S ENTERTAINMENT

Jonathan Houseman Davis, lead singer of Korn, was born a Presbyterian, but converted to Catholicism because his mother wanted to marry his stepfather in a Catholic church.

Nick Mason is the only member of Pink Floyd to appear on all of the band's albums.

Spencer Eldon was the name of the naked baby on the cover of Nirvana's album *Nevermind*.

The 80s song 'Rosanna' was written by Rosanna Arquette, the actress.

The B52s, were named after a fifties hairdo.

The bagpipe was originally made from the whole skin of a dead sheep.

The band Duran Duran got their name from an astronaut in the 1968 Jane Fonda movie *Barbarella*.

THAT'S ENTERTAINMENT

■ The Beach Boys formed in 1961.

■ The Beatles featured two left-handed members: Paul, whom everyone saw holding his Hoffner bass left-handed, and Ringo, whose left-handedness is at least partially to blame for his 'original' drumming style.

■ The Beatles performed their first US concert in Carnegie Hall.

■ The Beatles song 'A Day in the Life' ends with a note sustained for 40 seconds.

■ The Beatles song 'Dear Prudence' was written about Mia Farrow's sister Prudence, when she wouldn't come out and play with Mia and the Beatles at a religious retreat in India.

■ The biggest selling Christmas single of all time is Bing Crosby's 'White Christmas'.

THAT'S ENTERTAINMENT

The first CD pressed in the US was Bruce Springsteen's *Born in the USA*.

The Grateful Dead were once called 'The Warlocks'.

The harmonica is the world's most popular instrument.

The horse's name in the song 'Jingle Bells' is Bobtail.

The licence plate number that appears on the Volkswagon that appeared on the cover of the Beatles' *Abbey Road* album was 281F.

The Mamas and Papas were once called the Mugwumps.

The only member of the band ZZ Top to not have a beard has the last name Beard.

There is a music band named 'A Life-Threatening Buttocks Condition'.

THAT'S ENTERTAINMENT

■ The song with the longest title is 'I'm a Cranky Old Yank in a Clanky Old Tank on the Streets of Yokohama with my Honolulu Mama Doin' Those Beat-o, Beat-o Flat-On-My-Seat-o, Hirohito Blues' written by Hoagy Carmichael. He later claimed the song title ended with 'Yank' and the rest was a joke.

■ Tommy James was in a New York hotel looking at the Mutual of New York building's neon sign flashing repeatedly: M-O-N-Y. He suddenly got the inspiration to write his #1 hit 'Mony Mony'.

■ 'When I'm Sixty-Four' was the first song to be recorded for the *Sgt. Pepper* album. 'Within You Without You' was the last.

■ When John Lennon divorced Julian Lennon's mother Cynthia, Paul McCartney composed 'Hey Jude' to cheer Julian up.

THAT'S ENTERTAINMENT

ABBA got their name by taking the first letter from each of their names (Agnetha, Bjorn, Benny, Anni-frid).

Caruso and Roy Orbison were the only tenors this century capable of hitting 'e' over high 'c'.

The song, 'I am the Walrus', by John Lennon was inspired by a police two-tone siren.

There are more than 33,000 radio stations around the world.

One in every four Americans has appeared on television.

60.2 per cent of the US TV audience watched the final episode of *M*A*S*H* in 1983.

As well as appearing in *Star Trek*, William Shatner, Leonard Nimoy, James Doohan and George Takei have all appeared at one time or another on *The Twilight Zone*.

THAT'S ENTERTAINMENT

■ Captain Jean-Luc Picard's fish was named Livingston.

■ Daytime dramas are called soap operas because they were originally used to advertise soap powder. In America in the early days of TV, advertisers would write stories around the use of their soap powder.

■ For many years, the globe on the *NBC Nightly News* spun in the wrong direction. On 2 January 1984, NBC finally set the world spinning back in the proper direction.

■ In *Gilligan's Island*, the Professor's real name was Roy Hinkley, Mary Ann's last name was Summers and Mrs Howell's maiden name was Wentworth.

■ Hawkeye on the TV series *M*A*S*H* had the TV name of Benjamin Franklin Pierce. The actor's name was Alan Alda.

THAT'S ENTERTAINMENT

If you pause *Saturday Night Fever* at the 'How Deep Is Your Love' rehearsal scene, you will see the camera crew reflected in the dance hall mirror.

In every episode of *Seinfeld* there is a Superman somewhere.

In the theme song from *The Flintstones*, the line after 'Let's ride with the family down the street' is 'through the courtesy of Fred's two feet!'.

Jamie Farr (who played Klinger on Mash) was the only member of the cast who actually served as a soldier in the Korean War.

M*A*S*H stood for 'Mobile Army Surgical Hospital'.

Mr Munster's first name is Herman.

Mr Spock was second in command of the Starship Enterprise.

THAT'S ENTERTAINMENT

Mr Spock's blood type was T-Negative.

On the Roseanne show, DJ stood for David Jacob.

One of the many Tarzans, Karmuala Searlel, was mauled to death by a raging elephant on the set.

TV sitcom characters rarely say goodbye when they hang up the phone.

The actor who played Wedge in the original *Star Wars* trilogy has a famous nephew: actor Ewan McGregor, who plays young Obi-Wan in the new *Star Wars* film.

The Brady Brunch went to elementary school at Dixie Canyon Elementary.

The characters Bert and Ernie on *Sesame Street* were named after Bert the cop and Ernie the taxi driver in Frank Capra's *Its A Wonderful Life*.

THAT'S ENTERTAINMENT

■ The first crime mentioned in the first episode of *Hill Street Blues* was armed robbery.

■ The first ever televised murder case appeared on TV in 1955, 5–9 December. The accused was Harry Washburn.

■ The name of the 'Love Boat' was the *Pacific Princess*.

■ The wheel on the game show '*Wheel of Fortune*' is 102 inches in diameter.

■ There are as many as 78 scenes in a single *X-Files* episode.

■ TV's top-rated series from 1957 to 1961 was *Gunsmoke*.

■ 'Video Killed the Radio Star' was the very first video ever played on MTV.

FOOD AND DRINK

FOOD AND DRINK

400 quarter-pounders can be made out of one cow.

Seven per cent of Americans eat McDonalds each day.

A can of Diet Coke will float in water while a can of regular Coke sinks.

A can of SPAM is opened every four seconds.

A chili pepper isn't a pepper. In fact, more than two hundred kinds of chili peppers aren't peppers.

A company in Taiwan makes dinnerware out of wheat, so you can eat your plate.

A full seven per cent of the entire Irish barley crop goes to the production of Guinness beer.

A hard-boiled egg will spin. An uncooked or soft-boiled egg will not.

FOOD AND DRINK

A man named Ed Peterson is the inventor of the Egg McMuffin.

A Saudi Arabian women can get a divorce if her husband doesn't give her coffee.

Almonds are a member of the peach family.

Almonds are the oldest, most widely cultivated and extensively used nuts in the world.

Almost 425,000 hotdogs and buns, 160,000 hamburgers and cheeseburgers were served at Woodstock '99.

Americans on average eat 18 acres of pizza every day.

As much as 50 gallons of Maple Sap are used to make a single gallon of Maple Sugar.

FOOD AND DRINK

Astronauts are not allowed to eat beans before they go into space because passing wind in a spacesuit damages them.

At McDonald's in New Zealand, they serve apricot pies instead of cherry ones.

Beer foam will go down if you lick your finger then stick it in the beer.

■ Blueberry Jelly Bellies were created especially for Ronald Reagan.

Bubble gum contains rubber.

California's Frank Epperson invented the Popsicle in 1905 when he was 11 years old.

Chefs started using onions 5,000 years ago to spice up their cooking.

Chewing gum while peeling onions will keep you from crying.

Chewing gum is made from chicle.

FOOD AND DRINK

Chilli powder today is typically a blend of dried chillis, garlic powder, red peppers, oregano and cumin.

China produces 278,564,356,980 eggs per year.

China's Beijing Duck Restaurant can seat 9,000 people at one time.

Coca-Cola owns the world's second largest truck fleet.

Coca-Cola was first served in Atlanta, USA (Jacob's Pharmacy) in 1886 for only 5 cents a glass. The formula for Coca-Cola was created by pharmacist John Pemberton.

Coca-Cola was originally green.

Coffee does not help sober up a drunk person. In many cases it may actually increase the adverse effects of alcohol.

Coffee is the second largest item of international commerce in the world.

FOOD AND DRINK

Coffee is the world's most popular stimulant.

Coke is used to clean up blood spills on highways.

Cooking destroys the eyewatering agent.

Crack gets its name because it crackles when you smoke it.

Cranberry jelly is the only jelly flavour that comes from the real fruit, not artificial flavouring.

Diet Coke was only invented in 1983.

Dogs and cats consume over $11 billion worth of pet food a year. (Source: N/A)

Doughnuts originated in Holland.

Dry cereal for breakfast was invented by John Henry Kellogg at the turn of the century.

FOOD AND DRINK

Dunkin' Donuts serves about 112,500 doughnuts each day.

During your lifetime you will eat 60,000 pounds of food, the weight of six elephants.

Each year, Americans spend more on cat food than on baby food.

Earl Dean developed the bottle design for Coca-Cola.

Fanta Orange is the third largest selling soft drink in the world.

Five jelly flavours that flopped: celery, coffee, cola, apple and chocolate.

Fortune cookies were actually invented in America, in 1918, by Charles Jung.

France has the highest per capita consumption of cheese.

George Washington Carver invented peanut butter.

FOOD AND DRINK

■ Honey is used as a centre for golf balls and in antifreeze mixtures.

■ Ice cream was originally made without sugar and eggs.

■ If China imported just 10 per cent of its rice needs the price on the world market would increase by 80 per cent.

■ If you put a raisin in a glass of champagne, it will keep floating to the top and sinking to the bottom.

■ In 1865 opium was grown in the state of Virginia and a product was distilled from it that yielded four per cent morphine. In 1867 it was grown in Tennessee; six years later it was cultivated in Kentucky. During these years opium, marijuana and cocaine could be purchased legally over the counter from any chemist.

■ In 1983, a Japanese artist made a copy of the *Mona Lisa* completely out of toast.

FOOD AND DRINK

■ In 1989, Pepsi came out with a morning soft drink called 'Pepsi AM'. It didn't last long on the market.

■ In Australia, the number one topping for pizza is eggs. In Chile, the favourite topping is mussels and clams. In the United States, it's pepperoni.

■ In cooking, six drops make a dash.

■ In the summer, walnuts get a tan.

■ It is estimated that Americans will consume 10 million tons of turkey on Thanksgiving Day. Due to turkey's high sulphur content, Americans will also produce enough gas to fly a fleet of 75 Hindenburghs from LA to New York in 24 hours.

■ It takes more than 500 peanuts to make one 12-ounce jar of peanut butter.

■ Japan is the largest exporter of frogs' legs.

⁻OOD AND DRINK

Jelly Belly jelly beans were the first jelly beans in outer space when they went up with astronauts in the 21 June, 1983 voyage of the space shuttle Challenger.

Ketchup originated in China.

Laws forbidding the sale of sodas on Sunday prompted William Garwood to invent the ice cream sundae in Evanston, IL, in 1875.

Less than 3 per cent of Nestle's sales are for chocolate.

M&M's stands for the last names of Forrest Mars Sr., the sweet maker, and his associate Bruce Murrie.

M&M's were developed so soldiers could eat the sweets without getting their fingers sticky.

FOOD AND DRINK

Mexican jumping beans jump because of a moth larva inside the bean.

More popcorn is sold in Dallas than anywhere else in the United States.

More than half of the different types of cheese in the world come from France.

Muffins spelled backwards is sniffum.

Nicotine was introduced by Jean Nicot (French Ambassador to Portugal) in France in 1560.

No two cornflakes look the same.

Britain's most popular snack food is potato crisps.

Nutmeg is extremely poisonous if injected intravenously.

One of the ingredients in some ice cream is seaweed.

FOOD AND DRINK

■ One of the reasons marijuana is illegal today is because cotton growers in the 30s lobbied against hemp farmers – they saw it as competition. It is not chemically addictive as is nicotine, alcohol, or caffeine.

■ Only five per cent of salt produced ends up on the dinner table. The rest is used for packing meat, building roads, feeding livestock, tanning leather and manufacturing glass, soap, ash and washing compounds.

■ The only food that does not spoil is honey.

■ Orange juice helps the body absorb iron easily when consumed with a meal.

■ Peanuts are cholesterol free.

■ Peanuts are one of the ingredients of dynamite.

FOOD AND DRINK

People spend a lot more money on groceries when they shop on a hungry stomach.

Pepsi is commonly used by wooden boat owners to clean mould from decks. You can spill it on for about 30 seconds, but it needs rinsing to make sure it does not erode your decks completely.

Pepsi originally contained pepsin, therefore the name.

Potato crisps were invented in Louisiana in 1853.

Potatoes were first imported by Europe in the 1500s on Spanish ships returning from Peru.

Pound cake is called 'pound' cake because the original recipe required one pound of butter.

Pound for pound, hamburgers cost more than new cars.

FOOD AND DRINK

Reindeer milk has more fat than cow milk.

Researchers in Denmark found that beer tastes best when drunk to the accompaniment of a certain musical tone. The optimal frequency is different for each beer, they reported. The correct harmonious tone for Carlsberg lager, for example, is 510–520 cycles per second.

Rice is grown on more than 10 per cent of the earth's farmable surface.

Rice is the main food for half of the people of the world.

Rice is thrown at weddings as a symbol of fertility.

Salt is one of the few spices that is all taste and no smell.

Salt is the only rock humans can eat.

Saturday night is the biggest night of the week for eating pizza.

FOOD AND DRINK

Sheep's milk is used to produce Roquefort cheese.

Shredded Wheat was the first ready-to-eat breakfast cereal.

■ Since 1978, at least 37 people have died as a result of shaking vending machines, in an attempt to get free merchandise. More than 100 have been injured.

■ Small flat icebergs have been fitted with sails and piloted more than 2,400 miles from the Antarctic to Valparaiso, Chile, and to Cakkaiub, Peru.

Some people drink the urine of pregnant women to build up their immune system.

Some people like to chew sugar when they chew gum.

FOOD AND DRINK

■ Tabasco sauce is made by fermenting vinegar and hot peppers in a French oak barrel which has three inches of salt on top and is aged for three years until all the salt is diffused through the barrel.

■ Table salt is the only commodity that hasn't risen dramatically in price in the last 150 years.

■ The amount of potato crisps Americans eat each year weighs six times more than the *Titanic*.

■ The average American chews 190 sticks of gum, drinks 600 sodas and 800 gallons of water, eats 135 pounds of sugar and 19 pounds of cereal per year.

■ The biggest selling restaurant food is french fries.

■ The Bloody Mary is known as the 'Queen of Drinks'. and was invented in Harry's Bar, Paris in the 1930s.

FOOD AND DRINK

The chocolate chip cookie was invented in 1933.

The citrus soda 7-UP was created in 1929; 7 was selected because the original containers were 7 ounces. UP indicated the direction of the bubbles.

The colour of a chilli is no indication of its spiciness, but size usually is – the smaller the pepper, the hotter it is.

The dark meat on a roast turkey has more calories than the white meat.

The English word 'soup' comes from the Middle Ages word 'sop,' which means a slice of bread over which roast drippings were poured.

The estimated number of M&M's sold each day in the United States is 200 million.

The fat molecules in goat's milk are five times smaller than those found in cow's milk.

FOOD AND DRINK

The first man to distill bourbon whiskey was a Baptist preacher in 1789.

The first western consumer product sold in the old Soviet Union was Pepsi-Cola.

The food of the Greek gods was called Ambrosia.

The glue on Israeli postage stamps is certified kosher.

The heat of peppers is rated on the Scoville scale.

■ The highest lifetime yield of milk for a single cow is 465,224lbs.

The hottest chile in the world is the habanero.

The largest apple pie ever baked was 40 by 23 feet.

The largest hamburger in the world weighed in at 5,520 pounds.

FOOD AND DRINK

The largest ketchup bottle is a 170 feet (52m) water tower.

The liquid inside young coconuts can be used as a substitute for blood plasma in an emergency.

The McDonalds at The Skydome in Toronto, Ontario, is the only one in the world that sells hot dogs.

The most popular ice cream flavour is vanilla.

The most popular sweet pepper is the bell pepper.

The number 57 on a Heinz ketchup bottle represents the number of varieties of pickle the company once had.

The only real food US astronauts are allowed in space are pecan nuts.

The Southern dish 'chitlins' is made up of pigs' small intestines.

OOD AND DRINK

The top layer of a wedding cake, known as the groom's cake, is usually a fruit cake so it will last until the couple's first anniversary, when they will eat it.

The US Government spent $277,000 on 'Pickle research' in 1993.

The wheat that produces a one-pound loaf of bread requires two tons of water to grow.

The world's number one producer and consumer of fresh pork is China.

There are 2 million different combinations of sandwiches that can be created from a SUBWAY menu.

There are more donut shops per capita in Canada than in any other country.

There are more than 100 chemicals in one cup of coffee.

There are more than 15,000 different kinds of rice.

FOOD AND DRINK

There are only two people in the world that know the secret recipe for Coca-Cola.

There is cyanide in apple pips.

There is no such thing as blue food, even blueberries are purple.

Too much caffeine can cause heart palpitations.

Vanilla is used to make chocolate.

Virginia Woolfe wrote all her books standing up.

When a coffee seed is planted, it takes five years to yield consumable fruit.

When honey is swallowed, it enters the blood stream within a period of 20 minutes.

FOOD AND DRINK

Widows of a recently deceased king among the Baganda people of Uganda, have the honour of drinking the beer in which the king's entrails have been cleaned.

Wine will spoil if exposed to light, hence tinted bottles.

Worcestershire sauce is basically an anchovy ketchup.

Yogurt intake among North Americans has quadrupled in the past 20 years.

You should not eat a crayfish with a straight tail. It was dead before it was cooked.

There are more brown M&M's in plain M&M's than in peanuts.

16,850 bananas are eaten each week in the Boston University dining room.

Bananas do not grow on trees, but on rhizomes.

FOOD AND DRINK

Cranberries are sorted for ripeness by bouncing them; a fully ripened cranberry can be dribbled like a basketball.

Fresh apples float because 25 per cent of their volume is air.

Grapes explode when you put them in the microwave.

In Ivrea, Italy, thousands of citizens celebrate the beginning of Lent by throwing oranges at one another.

Lemons contain more sugar than strawberries.

Over 200 varieties of watermelon are grown in the US.

Over a third of all pineapples come from Hawaii.

Pineapples do not ripen after they have been picked.

Pomology is the study of fruit.

FOOD AND DRINK

Seeds are missing from a navel orange.

The average banana weighs 126 grams.

The avocado has the most calories of any fruit.

The bigger the navel the sweeter the orange.

The most widely eaten fruit in America is the banana.

Tomatoes and cucumbers are fruits.

Beijing boasts the world's largest Kentucky Fried Chicken restaurant.

In a typical restaurant, customers receive 27 pence worth of food for each pound they spend.

On average there are 178 sesame seeds on each McDonald's BigMac bun.

90 per cent of vitamin C in brussels sprouts will be lost in cooking.

FOOD AND DRINK

Ray Kroc bought McDonalds for $2.7 million in 1961 from the McDonald brothers.

Ninety-six per cent of a cucumber is water.

Apples, not caffeine, are more efficient for waking you up in the morning.

Brussel sprouts are called brussel sprouts because they were discovered in Brussels.

Eating raw onions is good for unblocking a stuffed nose.

Eggplant is a member of the thistle family.

Onions are low in calories and a good source of vitamin C, calcium, potassium and fibre.

Onions get their distinctive smell by soaking up sulphur from the soil.

FOOD AND DRINK

Onions help circulation.

Pumpkins contain vitamin A and potassium.

The most common pear world-wide is the Bartlett. It is bell-shaped, sweet and soft with a light green colour.

The oldest known vegetable is the pea.

'Tomatina' is the legendary Spanish tomato-throwing festival.

Turnips turn green when sunburned.

You use more calories eating celery than there are in celery itself.

Carbonated water, with nothing else in it, can dissolve limestone, talc and many other low-Moh's hardness minerals. Coincidentally, carbonated water is the main ingredient in soda pop.

FOOD AND DRINK

■ Drinking water after eating reduces the acid in your mouth by 61 per cent.

■ Drinking water is about three billion years old.

■ Forty-eight million people in the United States receive their drinking water from private or household wells.

■ H_2O expands as it freezes and contracts as it melts, displacing the exact same amount of fluid in either state. So if the northern ice cap did melt, it would cause absolutely no rise in the level of the ocean.

■ Hot water is heavier than cold.

■ In the typical Canadian home, 45 per cent of water is used for the toilet, 28 per cent is used for bathing and personal matters, 23 per cent is used for laundry or dishes and four per cent is used for cooking or drinking purposes.

FOOD AND DRINK

■ It takes about a half a gallon of water to cook macaroni, and about a gallon to clean the pot.

■ It's impossible to get water out of a rimless tyre.

■ Less than two per cent of the water on earth is fresh.

■ There is a tea in China called white tea which is simply boiled water.

WORLD OF BUSINESS

WORLD OF BUSINESS

■ A single share of Coca-Cola stock, purchased in 1919, when the company went public, would have been worth $92,500 in 1997.

■ IBM's motto is 'Think'.

■ It takes about 63,000 trees to make the newsprint for the average Sunday edition of *The New York Times*.

■ NERF, the popular foam children's toy company, doesn't actually stand for anything.

■ Nestlé is the largest company in Switzerland, yet more than 98 per cent of its revenue comes from outside the country.

■ Organized crime is estimated to account for 10% of the United States' national income.

WORLD OF BUSINESS

■ Sixty per cent of big-firm executives say the cover letter is as important or more important than the résumé itself when you're looking for a new job.

■ The three most valuable brand names on earth are Marlboro, Coca-Cola, and Budweiser, in that order.

■ The average bank cashier loses £175 a year.

■ The largest employer in the world is the Indian railway system, employing over a million people.

■ The most dangerous job in the United States is that of sanitation worker. Fire fighters and police officers are a close second and third, followed by leather tanners in fourth.

■ The sale of vodka makes up 10 per cent of Russian Government income.

WORLD OF BUSINESS

■ The slogan on New Hampshire licence plates is 'Live Free or Die'. These licence plates are manufactured by prisoners in the state prison in Concord.

■ Workers at Matsushita Electric Company in Japan beat dummies of their foremen with bamboo sticks to let off steam. The company has enjoyed 30 per cent growth for 25 consecutive years.

THE LITERARY WORLD

THE LITERARY WORLD

Bambi was originally published in 1929 in German.

During his entire lifetime, Herman Melville's timeless classic of the sea *Moby Dick*, only sold 50 copies.

General Lew Wallace's bestseller *Ben Hur* was the first work of fiction to be blessed by a pope.

Guinness Book of Records holds the record for being the book most often stolen from public libraries.

In 1898 (14 years prior to the *Titanic* tragedy), Morgan Robertson wrote a novel called *Futility*. This fictitious novel was about the largest ship ever built hitting an iceberg in the Atlantic ocean on a cold April night.

Keeping Warm With an Axe is the title of a real how-to book.

Mary Shelley wrote *Frankenstein* at the age of 19.

THE LITERARY WORLD

People in Iceland read more books per capita than any other people in the world.

The all time bestselling electronic book is Stephen King's *Riding The Bullet*.

The Bible is the number one shoplifted book in America.

The book of Esther in the Bible is the only book which does not mention the name of God.

The only person to decline a Pulitzer Prize for Fiction was Sinclair Lewis for his book *Arrowsmith*.

Tom Sawyer was the first novel written on a typewriter.

A 'prestidigitator' is another word for magician.

A castrated rooster is called a capon.

THE LITERARY WORLD

A conehologist studies molluscs and shells.

A deltiologist collects postcards.

A fingerprint is also known as a dactylogram.

A funambulist is a tightrope walker.

A group of bears is called a sleuth.

A group of kittens is called a kindle.

A gynaephobic man fears women.

A horologist measures time.

A klazomaniac is someone who feels like shouting.

A librocubicularist is someone who reads in bed.

A phonophobe fears noise.

THE LITERARY WORLD

A phrenologist feels and interprets skull features.

A sultan's wife is called a sultana.

Acrophobia is the fear of heights.

An anthropophagist eats people.

Carcinomaphobia is the fear of cancer.

Certain sounds in the English language are real germ spreaders, particularly the sounds of F, P, T, D and S.

Killing a king is called regicide.

Narcissism is the psychiatric term for self-love.

Nyctohylophobia is the fear of dark wooded areas, of forests at night.

Of all the words in the English language, the word 'set' has the most definitions.

THE LITERARY WORLD

Paedophobia is a fear of children.

Patty & Selma, from *The Simpsons*, smoke 'Laramie' brand cigarettes.

Pyrophobia is the fear of fire.

Rhythm and syzygy are the longest English words without vowels.

Scuba stands for 'Self-contained underwater breathing apparatus'.

Sheriff came from Shire Reeve. During early years of feudal rule in England, each shire had a reeve who was the law for that shire. When the term was taken to the United States it was shortened to sheriff.

Skepticisms is the longest typed word that alternates hands.

Spat-out food is called chanking.

THE LITERARY WORLD

Taphephobia is the fear of being buried alive.

Telephonophobia is the fear of telephones.

The ball on top of a flagpole is called the truck.

The fox's tail is called a brush.

The letter J does not appear anywhere on the periodic table of elements.

The letter W is the only letter in the alphabet that doesn't have one syllable, it has three.

The longest one-syllable word in the English language is screeched.

The longest word in the English language is 1909 letters long and it refers to a distinct part of DNA.

The meaning of 'stool pigeon' is an informer or a traitor.

THE LITERARY WORLD

The most common letters in the English language are R, S, T, L, N, and E.

The most used letter in the English alphabet is E, and Q is the least used.

The Old English word for sneeze is *fneosam*.

The oldest word in the English language is town.

The only 15-letter word that can be spelled without repeating a letter is uncopyrightable.

The only contemporary words that end with gry are angry and hungry.

The phrase 'rule of thumb' is derived from an old English law stating that you cannot beat your wife with anything wider than your thumb.

THE LITERARY WORLD

The phrase sleep tight originated when mattresses were set upon ropes woven through the bed frame. To remedy sagging ropes, one would use a bed key to tighten the rope.

The term potty comes from the pint-sized chamber pot built for children.

The two ends of a magnet are called poles.

The U in U-boats stands for 'under water'.

The word constipation comes from a Latin word that means 'to crowd together'.

The word curfew originates from an old French word that means 'cover fire'.

The word diastima is the word for having a gap between your teeth.

The word lethologica describes the state of not remembering the word you want to say.

THE LITERARY WORLD

■ The word noon came from an old church term 'none' meaning three. There was a monastic order that was so devout that they declared they would not eat until that time. Since they rang the bells indicating time, none came earlier and earlier. The towns people called midday noon to ridicule them.

■ The word racecar and kayak are palindromes: the same whether they are read left to right or right to left.

■ The word rodent comes from the Latin word *rodere* meaning to gnaw.

■ The word samba means to rub navels together.

■ The words assassination and bump were invented by Shakespeare.

THE LITERARY WORLD

■ The world's longest name is Adolph Blaine Charles Daivid Earl Frederick Gerald Hubert Irvin John Kenneth Lloyd Martin Nero Oliver Paul Quincy Randolph Sherman Thomas Uncas Victor William Xerxes Yancy Zeus Wolfeschlegelsteinhausenbergerdorft Sr.

■ There are only four words in the English language which end in -dous: tremendous, horrendous, stupendous and hazardous.

■ There are only three world capitals that begin with the letter O in English: Ottawa, Canada; Oslo, Norway; and Ouagadougou, Burkina Faso.

■ There are six words in the English language with the letter combination uu. Muumuu, vacuum, continuum, duumvirate, duumvir and residuum.

■ There are 10 body parts that are only three letters long: eye, ear, leg, arm, jaw, gum, toe, lip, hip and rib.

THE LITERARY WORLD

There was no punctuation until the 15th century.

Tonsurphobia is the fear of haircuts.

When two words are combined to form a single word (e.g. motor + hotel = motel, breakfast + lunch = brunch) the new word is called a portmanteau.

When your sink is full, the little hole that lets the water drain, instead of flowing over the side, is called a porcelator.

Women who wink at men are known as 'nictitating' women.

Xenophobia is the fear of strangers or foreigners.

You would have to count to one thousand to use the letter A in the English language to spell a whole number.

Zoophobia is the fear of animals.

THE LITERARY WORLD

■ 1961 was the most recent year that could be written upside-down and right side-up and appear the same. The next year that this will be possible will be 6009!

■ 2,488,200 books will be shipped in the next 12 months with the wrong cover.

■ A 17th-century Swedish philologist claimed that in the Garden of Eden God spoke Swedish, Adam spoke Danish and the serpent spoke French.

■ A baby eel is called an elver; a baby oyster is called a spat.

■ A coward was originally a boy who took care of cows.

■ A Flemish artist is responsible for the world's smallest painting in history. It is a picture of a miller and his mill, and it was painted on to a grain of corn.

THE LITERARY WORLD

A group of crows is called a murder.

A group of officers is called a mess.

A hamlet is a village without a church and a town is not a city until it has a cathedral.

A hydrodaktulpsychicharmonica is a variety of musical glass.

A lump of pure gold the size of a matchbox car can be flattened into a sheet the size of a tennis court.

A necropsy is an autopsy on animals.

A poem written to celebrate a wedding is called a epithalamium.

A postcard collector is called a deltiologist.

A scholar who studies the Marquis de Sade is called a Sadian not a Sadist.

THE LITERARY WORLD

According to Douglas Adams, a salween is the faint taste of dishwashing liquid in a cup of fresh tea.

According to Genesis 1:20 – 22, the chicken came before the egg.

All Hebrew originating names that end with the letters 'el' have something to do with God.

Alma mater means bountiful mother.

Amphibious is based upon Greek words that mean living a double life; amphibians live in both land and water.

An animal epidemic is called an epizootic.

Arachibutyrophobia is the fear of peanut butter sticking to the roof of your mouth.

Arnold Schonberg suffered from triskaidecphobia, the fear of the number 13. He died 13 minutes from midnight on Friday the 13th.

THE LITERARY WORLD

Ballroom dancing is a major at Brigham University.

Before the turn of the century, the papers were called tabloids, chronicles, gazettes, etc. Most had local stories and far away stories were quite old as it took a while for stories to travel (and of course they were subject to changes from hand to hand. With the event of the teletype, stories could be broadcast all over at unheard of speed. Several of the papers started carrying a section with stories from all over - North, East, West & South and that's why they are called newspapers.

Bookkeeper is the only word in the English language with three consecutive double letters.

Chevrolet tried marketing a Chevrolet Nova in Spanish – speaking countries – it didn't sell well because NO VA means 'doesn't go' in Spanish.

THE LITERARY WORLD

Clans long ago that wanted to get rid of their unwanted people without killing them used to burn down their houses – hence the expression get fired.

Cleveland spelled backwards is DNA level C.

Clinophobia is the fear of beds.

Corduroy comes from the French, *cord du roi* or 'cloth of the king'.

Degringolade means to fall and disintegrate.

Dendrology is the study of trees.

Dibble means to drink like a duck.

Dr Seuss coined the word nerd in his 1950 book *If I Ran The Zoo*.

Dr Seuss pronounced his name so that it would rhyme with rejoice.

THE LITERARY WORLD

During his entire life, Vincent Van Gogh sold only one painting, *Red Vineyard at Arles*.

Dutch painter Vincent Van Gogh cut off his left ear. His *Self-portrait with the Bandaged Ear* shows the right one bandaged because he painted the mirror image.

EEG stands for Electroencephalogram.

EMI stands for 'Electrical and Musical Instrument'.

Entomophobia is the fear of insects.

Eosophobia is the fear of dawn.

Ernest Vincent Wright wrote the 50,000 – word novel *Gatsby* without any word containing 'e'.

Essay in French means 'to try, attempt'.

THE LITERARY WORLD

■ Ever wonder where the phrase 'two bits' came from? Some coins used in the American colonies before the Revolutionary War were Spanish dollars, which could be cut into pieces, or bits. Since two pieces equalled one-quarter dollar, the expression two bits came into being as a name for 25 cents.

■ Every minute 47 Bibles are sold or distributed throughout the world.

■ Facetious and abstemious contain all the vowels in the correct order, as does arsenious, meaning containing arsenic.

■ Fido means 'faithful' in Latin.

■ For much of the way, the Lewis and Clark expedition was led by a woman, Sacagawea, a Shoshone Indian. That's where that saying came from ... 'Behind every successful man, there is a woman with a road map'.

THE LITERARY WORLD

■ For the 66 per cent of Americans who admit to reading in the bathroom, the preferred reading material is '*Reader's Digest*'.

■ Forget-me-not: According to German legend this flower gets its name from the last words of a knight, who was drowned while trying to pick some from the riverside for his lady.

■ German is considered the sister language of English.

■ Ghosts appear in four Shakespearian plays; *Julius Caesar, Richard III, Hamlet* and *Macbeth*.

■ Goethe couldn't stand the sound of barking dogs and could only write if he had an apple rotting in the drawer of his desk.

THE LITERARY WORLD

■ Great Britain was the first county to issue postage stamps. Hence, the postage stamps of Britain are the only stamps in the world not to bear the name of the country of origin. However, every stamp carries a relief image or a silhouette of the monarch's head instead.

■ Groaking is to watch people eating in the hope that they will offer you some.

■ Ham radio operators got the term 'ham' coined from the expression 'ham-fisted operators,' a term used to describe early radio users who sent Morse code (i.e pounded their fists).

■ Happy as a clam is from the expression 'happy as a clam at high tide'. Clams are only harvested when the tide is out.

■ Hara kiri is an impolite way of saying the Japanese word *seppuku* which means, literally, belly splitting.

THE LITERARY WORLD

■ Hawaiian words do not contain consonant clusters. For example, Kahlua is not a Hawaiian word.

■ Hydroxydesoxycorticosterone and hydroxydeoxycorticosterones are the largest anagrams.

■ 'I am'. is the shortest complete sentence in the English language.

■ If each count were one second long, it would take about 12 days to count to a million and 32 years to count to a billion.

■ If you look carefully at the picture of the *Mona Lisa*, you will notice a bridge in the background.

■ Ignoramus: The grand jury used to write ignoramus on the back of indictments not found or not to be sent to court. This was often construed as an indication of the stupidity of the jury, hence its present meaning.

THE LITERARY WORLD

In England, in the 1880s pants was considered a dirty word.

In English, four is the only digit that has the same number of letters as its value.

In Ethiopia, both males and females of the Surma tribes shave their heads as a mark of beauty.

In Italy, a campaign for Schweppes Tonic Water translated the name into Schweppes Toilet Water.

In most advertisements, including newspapers, the time displayed on a watch is 10:10.

In Papua New Guinea, there are villages within five miles of each other which speak different languages.

In the 40s, the Bich pen was changed to Bic for fear that Americans would pronounce it 'Bitch'.

THE LITERARY WORLD

In the Philippines, *Mabuhey* means 'to bring life to'.

Influenza got its name from the fact that people believed the disease was because of the evil 'influence' of stars.

It is believed that Shakespeare was 46 around the time that the King James Version of the Bible was written. In Psalms 46, the 46th word from the first word is shake and the 46th word from the last word is spear.

It is possible to drown and not die. Technically the term 'drowning' refers to the process of taking water into the lungs, not to death caused by that process.

Ivanov is the most common Russian surname.

January is named after the Roman god Janus.

Jet lag was once called boat lag, before there were jets.

THE LITERARY WORLD

Karaoke means empty orchestra in Japanese.

Kemo Sabe means 'soggy shrub' in Navajo.

Koala is Aboriginal for no drink.

Lachanophobia is the fear of vegetables.

Lead poisoning is known as plumbism.

Libra, the scales, is the only inanimate symbol in the zodiac.

Linn's Stamp News is the world's largest weekly newspaper for stamp collectors.

MAFIA is an acronym for *Morte Alla Francia Italia Anela*, or Death to the French is Italy's Cry.

Maine is the only state whose name is just one syllable.

THE LITERARY WORLD

More than 26 dialects of Quichua are spoken in Ecuador.

Mothers were originally named mama or mommy (in many languages) because they have mammary glands.

Naked means to be unprotected; nude means unclothed.

Native speakers of Japanese learn Spanish more easily than English. Native speakers of English learn Spanish more easily than Japanese.

Nine is considered the luckiest number worldwide.

No word in the English language rhymes with month, orange, silver or purple.

Nova Scotia is Latin for New Scotland.

19 November is 'Have a Bad Day day'.

THE LITERARY WORLD

29 November is 'National Sinky Day', a day to eat over one's sink and worship it.

November when translated literally is the ninth month.

Nycrophobia is the fear of darkness.

10 October is National Metric Day.

Papaphobia is the fear of popes.

People didn't always say hello when they answered the phone. When the first regular phone service was established in 1878, people said Ahoy.

Phobatrivaphobia is fear of trivia about phobias.

Polish is the only word in the English language that when capitalized is changed from a noun or a verb to a nationality.

THE LITERARY WORLD

■ Put a sock in it: be quiet, shut-up, make less noise; a slang expression. In the late 19th century and earlier years of the 20th century, when gramophones or phonographs amplified the sound through large horns, woollen socks were often stuffed in them to cut down the noise.

■ Quisling is the only word in the English language to start with 'quis'.

■ Rio de Janeiro translates to River of January.

■ Scatologists are experts who study poop (aka crap, dung, dookie, dumps, faeces, excrement, etc.)

■ Sekkusu is sex in Japanese.

■ 'Smithee' is a pseudonym that filmmakers use when they don't want their names to appear in the credits.

THE LITERARY WORLD

■ Son of a gun: this familiar designation implying contempt but now used with jocular familiarity derives from the days when women were allowed to live in naval ships. The son of the gun was one born in the ship often near the midship gun, behind canvas screen. If the paternity was uncertain, the child was entered in the log as 'son of a gun'.

■ Spain literally means 'the land of rabbits'.

■ Stewardesses is the longest word that is typed with only the left hand.

■ Strange- but -real college courses offered advanced cereal science, amusement park administration, clay wheel throwing, fatherhood and soil judging.

■ The 'a.m.' in 5:00 a.m. stands for ante meridiem.

■ The 'you are here arrow' on a map is called the IDEO locator.

THE LITERARY WORLD

The third year of marriage is called the leather anniversary.

The abbreviation 'e.g.' stands for 'Exempli gratia', or 'For example.'

■ The abbreviation for one pound, lb, comes from the astrological sign Libra meaning balance.

■ The abbreviation ORD for Chicago's O'Hare airport comes from the old name Orchard Field.

■ The Bible has been translated into Klingon.

The correct response to the Irish greeting 'Top of the morning to you', is 'And the rest of the day to yourself'.

The 'D' in D-day means Day. The French term for 'D-Day' is 'J-jour'.

THE LITERARY WORLD

- The earliest document in Latin in a woman's handwriting (it is from the first century AD) is an invitation to a birthday party.

- The Eskimo language has over 20 words to describe different kinds of snow.

- The expletive 'Holy Toledo' refers to Toledo, Spain, which became an outstanding Christian cultural centre in 1085.

- The expression 'What in tarnation' comes from the original meaning 'What in eternal damnation'.

- The famous painting of *Whistler's Mother* was once bought from a pawn shop.

- The first issue of *People Magazine*, in 1974, cost 35 cents and featured actress Mia Farrow on the cover.

THE LITERARY WORLD

The French term 'bourrage de crane' for wartime propaganda means brain stuffing.

The heraldic term 'gules', meaning red, comes from the French word *gueules*, meaning a throat.

The infinity character on the keyboard is called a lemniscate.

The Japanese translation of switch is pronounced suitchi.

The Kentucky Fried Chicken slogan 'finger-lickin' good' came out as 'eat your fingers off' in Chinese.

The leading female singer in an opera is called the prima donna.

The letters KGB stand for Komitet Gosudarstvennoy Bezopasnos.

THE LITERARY WORLD

■ The longest place name still in use is: Taumatawhakatangihangaoauauotamete aturipukakapikimaungahoronukupokaiw- henuakitanatahu – a New Zealand hill.

■ The longest place name in Great Britain is that of a Welsh village: Gorsafawdda- chaidraigddanheddogleddollonpenrhynar eurdraethceredigion.

■ The magic word 'Abracadabra' was originally intended for the specific purpose of curing hay fever.

■ The metal part of a lamp that surrounds the bulb and supports the shade is called a harp.

■ The *Mona Lisa* painting was completed in 1503. It was stolen from the Louvre on August 21 1911.

■ The monastic hours are matins, lauds, prime, tierce, sext, nones, vespers and compline.

THE LITERARY WORLD

The most reverse charge calls are made on Father's Day.

The most common name for a goldfish is 'Jaws'.

The most common name in Italy is Mario Rossi.

The most common name in the world is Mohammed.

The most common Spanish surname is Garcia.

The most common surname in Sweden is Johansson.

The most difficult tongue-twister is 'The sixth sick Sheik's sixth sheep's sick'.

The most popular name for a boat in 1996 was *Serenity*.

THE LITERARY WORLD

The naked truth: the fable says that Truth and Falsehood went bathing; Falsehood came first out of the water and dressed herself in Truth's garments. Truth, unwilling to take those of Falsehood, went naked.

The name fez is Turkish for hat.

The name for fungal remains found in coal is sclerotinite.

The national anthem of Greece has 158 verses.

The national anthem of the Netherlands, 'Het Wilhelmus', is an acrostichon. The first letters of each of the 15 verses represent the name Willem Van Nassov.

The Netherlands and the United States both have anthems that do not mention their country's name.

The next-to-last event is the penultimate, and the second-to-last is the antepenultimate.

THE LITERARY WORLD

■ The nursery rhyme 'Ring A Roses'
is a rhyme about the plague. Infected
people with the plague would get red
circular sores (ring of roses); these
sores would smell very badly so
common folk would put flowers
on their bodies somewhere
inconspicuously, so that it would
cover the smell of the sores
(pocket full of posies).

■ The original story from *Tales of 1001
Arabian Nights* begins, 'Aladdin was a
little Chinese boy'.

■ The phrase 'Often a bridesmaid, but
never a bride' actually comes from
an advertisement for Listerine
mouthwash.

■ The phrase jet lag was once called boat
lag, back before airplanes existed.

THE LITERARY WORLD

■ *The Practitioner*, a British medical journal, has determined that bird-watching may be hazardous to your health. The magazine, in fact, has officially designated bird-watching a hazardous hobby, after documenting the death of a weekend bird-watcher who became so immersed in his subject that he grew oblivious to his surroundings and consequently was eaten by a crocodile.

■ The Sanskrit word for 'war' means 'desire for more cows.'

■ The sentence 'the quick brown fox jumps over the lazy dog' uses every letter in the English language.

■ The slang word crap comes from T. Crapper, the man who invented the modern toilet.

■ The slash character is called a virgule, or solidus. A URL uses slash characters, not back slash characters.

THE LITERARY WORLD

■ The Spanish word for Navy is 'Armada'.

■ The stress in Hungarian words always falls on the first syllable.

■ The symbol on the pound key is called anoctothorpe.

■ The term 'honeymoon' is derived from the Babylonians who declared mead, a honey-flavoured wine, the official wedding drink, stipulating that the bride's parents be required to keep the groom supplied with the drink for the month following the wedding.

■ The term 'cop' came from Constable on Patrol. It is from England.

■ The term 'devil's advocate' comes from the Roman Catholic church. When deciding if someone should be sainted, a devil's advocate is always appointed to give an alternative view.

THE LITERARY WORLD

■ The term 'mayday' used for signalling for help (after SOS) comes from the French *M'aidez*, which, pronounced Mayday and means help me.

■ The term 'the Boogey man will get you' comes from the Boogy people who still inhabit an area of Indonesia. These people still act as pirates today and attack ships that pass.

■ The three best-known western names in China: Jesus Christ, Richard Nixon and Elvis Presley.

■ The traditional symbol of the pawnbroker – three golden balls – is thought to be dervied from the coat of arms of the Medici family, who ruled the Italian city of Florence between the 15th and 16th centuries. The symbol was spread by the Lombards – Italian bankers, goldsmiths and moneylenders who set up businesses in medieval London.

THE LITERARY WORLD

The word 'kangaroo' means 'I don't know' in the language of Australian Aborigines. When Captain Cook approached natives of the Endeavor River tribe to ask what the strange animal was, he got 'kangaroo' for an answer.

The word 'Karate' means empty hand.

The word byte is a contraction of by eight.

The word accordion comes from the German word 'akkord,' which means 'agreement, harmony.'

The word Aloha is used as both a greeting and a farewell in Hawaii.

The word calendar comes from Latin and means 'to call out'.

The word hangnail comes from the Middle English: ang-(painful) + nail. Nothing to do with hanging.

THE LITERARY WORLD

■ There are about 5,000 different languages spoken on earth.

■ There are no Spanish words that begin with the letter W (except for those of American – English origin).

■ There are only 12 letters in the Hawaiian alphabet.

■ Three – dog night (attributed to Australian Aborigines) came about because on especially cold nights these nomadic people needed three dogs to keep from freezing.

■ Trabant is the German word for satellite.

THE LITERARY WORLD

■ Why are computer defects called bugs? In 1943, Navy officer Grace Hopper found a glitch in her computer. After investigating, she discovered the system had a bug – a real one. It turned out a moth had made its way into Hopper's computer. Though the word bug has meant fault or defect since as far back as the 1870s, Hopper's story is credited with making it the synonym of choice in the computer industry.

■ X-ray technology has shown there are three different versions of the *Mona Lisa* under the visible one.

■ Zorro means fox in Spanish.

HOUSEHOLD
TRIVIA

7

HOUSEHOLD TRIVIA

A coat hanger is 44 inches long if straightened.

4,000 people are injured by teapots every year.

A 60-minute cassette contains 565 feet of tape.

A dime has 118 ridges around the edge.

A good quality Persian rug which contains one million knots in every three square inches can last as long as 500 years.

A good typist can strike 20 keys in a second.

A person uses more household energy shaving with a hand razor at a sink (because of the water power, the water pump and so on) than he would by using an electric razor.

A quarter has 119 rigdes on its edge.

HOUSEHOLD TRIVIA

A toothpick is the object most often choked on by Americans.

A typical double mattress contains as many as two million house dust mites.

A wedding ring is generally exempt by law from inclusion among the assets in a bankruptcy estate. That means that a wedding ring can't be seized by creditors, no matter how much the bankrupt person owes.

According to a market research survey done some time ago, 68 per cent of consumers receiving junk mail actually open the envelopes.

According to one study, 24 per cent of lawns have some sort of lawn ornament.

All 50 states are listed across the top of the Lincoln Memorial on the back of the American $5 bill.

All hospitals in Singapore use Pampers nappies.

HOUSEHOLD TRIVIA

Aluminium is strong enough to support 90,000 pounds per square inch.

Americans spend $1.5 billion dollars every year on toothpaste.

An average of 200 million credit cards are used every day in the United States.

Approximately 30 billion cakes of Ivory Soap had been manufactured by 1990.

At the height of inflation in Germany in the early 1920s, one pound was equal to a quintillion German marks.

Camera shutter speed 'B' stands for bulb.

Colgate faced a big obstacle marketing toothpaste in Spanish-speaking countries. Colgate translates into the command 'go hang yourself'.

Cow is a Japanese brand of shaving foam.

HOUSEHOLD TRIVIA

■ Each king in a deck of playing cards represents a great king from history. Spades – King David; Clubs – Alexander the Great; Hearts – Charlemagne; and Diamonds – Julius Caesar.

■ Each of the suits on a deck of cards represents the four major pillars of the economy in the middle ages: heart represented the Church; spades represented the military; clubs represented agriculture; and diamonds represented the merchant class.

■ Each of us generate five pounds of rubbish a day; most of it is paper.

■ Every year, over 8,800 people injure themselves with a toothpick.

■ How valuable is the penny you found lying on the ground? If it takes just a second to pick it up a person could make £36.00 per hour just picking up pennies.

HOUSEHOLD TRIVIA

If done perfectly, any Rubik's cube combination can be solved in 17 turns.

If you lace your shoes from the inside to the outside, the fit will be snugger around your big toe.

In 1955, one-third of all watches sold were Timexes.

In 1977, Cairo only had 208,000 telephones and no telephone books.

In 1990, there were about 15,000 vacuum cleaner-related accidents in the US.

In every deck of cards, the King of Hearts is sticking his sword through his head. That's why he's often called the Suicide King.

In order for a deck of cards to be mixed up enough to play with properly, it should be shuffled at least seven times.

It takes a plastic container 50,000 years to start decomposing.

HOUSEHOLD TRIVIA

It's rumoured that sucking on a copper penny will cause a breathalyser to read 0.

Ivory bar soap floating was a mistake. They had been mixing the soap formula causing excess air bubbles that made it float. Customers wrote and told how much they loved that it floated, and it has floated ever since.

John F Kennedy's rocking chair was auctioned off for $442,000.

Johnson & Johnson's 'BAND-AID' brand adhesive bandages have been around for 75 years.

Ketchup is excellent for cleaning brass, especially tarnished or corroded brass.

Kleenex tissues were originally used as filters in gas masks.

Lang Martin balanced seven golf balls vertically without adhesive at Charlotte, NC on 9 February 1980.

HOUSEHOLD TRIVIA

Mixing Sani-Flush and Comet cleaners has been known to cause explosions.

More people use blue toothbrushes than red ones.

Mosquito repellants do not repel. They hide you. The spray blocks the mosquito's sensors so they do not know you are there.

Murphy's Oil Soap is the chemical most commonly used to clean elephants.

No piece of paper can be folded in half more than seven times.

On average, 100 people choke on ballpoint pens every year.

On average, there are 333 squares of toilet paper on a roll.

On the new American hundred dollar bill the time on the clock tower of Independence Hall is 4:10.

HOUSEHOLD TRIVIA

Oral-B is a combination of oral hygiene and the letter B, which stands for the word 'better.'

People in China sometimes use firecrackers around their homes as fire alarms.

Playing cards became the first paper currency of Canada in 1685, when the French governor used them to pay off some war debts.

Playing cards in India are round.

Q-TIPS Cotton Swabs were originally called Baby Gays.

Rubber bands last longer when refrigerated.

Scotch tape has been used as an anti-corrosive shield on the Goodyear Blimp.

HOUSEHOLD TRIVIA

Scotchgard is a combination of the words Scotch, meaning Scotsman, and a misspelling of guard, meaning to protect.

Some Eskimos have been known to use refrigerators to keep their food from freezing.

Some toothpastes contain antifreeze.

The ace of spades in a playing card deck symbolizes death.

The Australian $5, $10, $20, $50 and $100 notes are made out of plastic.

The average person looks at eight houses before buying one.

The average lead pencil will draw a line 35 miles long or write approximately 50,000 English words.

The average mouse pad is 8.75 inches by 7.5 inches.

HOUSEHOLD TRIVIA

The average woman consumes six pounds of lipstick in her lifetime.

The average women's handbag weighs three to five pounds.

The concave dish shape that a liquid takes on inside a glass or tube is called a meniscus.

The dial tone of a normal telephone is in the key F.

The diameter of the wire in a standard paper clip is one millimetre or about 0.04 inch.

The end of a hammer, opposite the striking end, is called a peen.

The face of a penny can hold thirty drops of water.

The first US coin to bear the words, 'United States of America' was a penny made in 1727. It was also inscribed with the plain-spoken motto: 'Mind your own business'.

HOUSEHOLD TRIVIA

The holes in fly swatters are used to lower air resistance.

The hundred billionth crayon made by Crayola was Perriwinkle Blue.

The list of ingredients that make up lipstick include fish scales.

The most popular contact lens colour is blue.

The opposite sides of a dice cube add up to seven.

The original fifty cent piece in Australian decimal currency had around $100 worth of silver in it before it was replaced with a less expensive 12-sided coin.

The plastic things on the end of shoelaces are called aglets.

The playing card 'nine of hearts' is considered the symbol of love.

HOUSEHOLD TRIVIA

The quartz crystal in your wristwatch vibrates 32,768 times a second.

The Ramses brand condom is named after the great Pharaoh Rameses II who fathered over 160 children.

The ridges on the sides of coins are called reeding or milling.

The side of a hammer is a cheek.

Bill Bowerman, founder of Nike, got his first shoe idea after staring at a waffle iron. He got the idea of using squared spikes to make shoes lighter.

Jeans were named after Genoa, Italy, where the first denim cloth was made.

Neck ties were first worn in Croatia. That's why they were called cravats (cro-vats).

North Americans spend almost $18 billion on footwear a year.

HOUSEHOLD TRIVIA

On average, most people button their shirts upwards.

The armhole in clothing is called an armsaye.

The bra Marilyn Monroe wore in the movie 'Some Like It Hot', was sold for $14,000.

The YKK on the zipper of your Levis stands for Yoshida Kogyo Kabushibibaisha, the world's largest zipper manufacturer.

Three teaspoons make up one tablespoon.

40,000 Americans are injured by toilets every year.

A flush toilet exists today that dates back to 2000 BC.

About a third of people flush while they are still sitting on the toilet.

HOUSEHOLD TRIVIA

Alaska has more outhouses than any other state in the USA.

In 1825, the first toilet was installed in the White House.

In true kingly fashion, Elvis passed away while sitting on the throne.

It has been recommended by dentists that a toothbrush be kept six feet away from a toilet to avoid airborne particles resulting from the flush.

Most toilets flush in E flat.

Poet Henry Wadsworth Longfellow was the first American to have plumbing installed in his house in 1840.

The first toilet ever seen on television was on *Leave it to Beaver*.

The Soviet Sukhoi-34 is the first strike fighter with a toilet in it.

HOUSEHOLD TRIVIA

Toilets in Australia flush counter clockwise.

Ninety-four per cent of all households in Belgium with children up to the age of 14 years own LEGO products.

Barbie's full name is Barbara Millicent Roberts.

Barbie's measurements if she were life-size: 5 feet 9 inches tall, 33-18-31½.

Five-thousandths of a millimeter is the tolerance of accuracy at the LEGO mould factories.

If you took a standard slinky and stretched it out it would measure 87 feet.

In 1946, the first TV toy commercial aired. It was for Mr Potato Head.

HOUSEHOLD TRIVIA

■ In 1980, Namco released PAC-MAN, the most popular video game (or arcade game) of all time. The original name was going to be PUCK MAN, but executives saw the potential for vandals to scratch out part of the P in the games marquee and labelling.

■ In 1981, a man had a heart attack after playing the game BERSERK – video gaming's only known fatality.

■ It takes an average of 48 to 100 tries to solve a rubix cube puzzle.

■ Slinkys were invented by an airplane mechanic; he was playing with engine parts and realized the possible secondary use of one of the springs.

■ The hula hoop was the biggest selling toy in 1957.

■ The Slinky is sold on every continent of the world except Antarctica.

HOUSEHOLD TRIVIA

■ The yo-yo originated in the Phillippines, where it is used as a weapon in hunting.

■ There are 42 dots on a pair of dice.

■ There are more Barbie dolls in Italy than there are Canadians in Canada.

■ Totally Hair Barbie is the best selling Barbie of all time.

■ When the divorce rate goes up in the United States, toy makers say the sale of toys also rises.

PLACES

8

PLACES

160 cars can drive side by side on the Monumental Axis in Brazil, the world's widest road.

All the dirt from the foundation to build the World Trade Center in NYC was dumped into the Hudson River to form the community now known as Battery City Park.

■ At April 2000, Hong Kong had 392,000 faxlines – one of the highest rates of business fax use in the world.

■ At Hancock Secondary School in Mississippi there is actually a McDonalds in the high school.

At one point, the Circus Maximus in Rome could hold up to 250,000 people.

Buckingham Palace has over 600 rooms.

PLACES

■ Built in 1697, the Frankford Avenue Bridge which crosses Pennypack Creek in Philadelphia is the oldest US bridge in continuous use.

■ Coney Island, the amusement park, has had three of its rides designated as New York City historical landmarks.

■ Construction on the Leaning Tower of Pisa began on 9 August, 1173.

■ Disneyland opened in 1955.

■ Due to precipitation, for a few weeks K2 is taller than Mt. Everest.

■ Harvard uses Yale brand locks on their buildings; Yale uses Best brand.

PLACES

■ If a statue in the park of a person on a horse has both front legs in the air, the person died in battle; if the horse has one front leg in the air, the person died as a result of wounds received in battle; if the horse has all four legs on the ground, the person died of natural causes.

■ If you bring a raccoon's head to the Henniker, New Hampshire town hall, you are entitled to receive $10 from the town.

■ If you come from Manchester, you are a Mancunian.

■ If you divide the Great Pyramid's perimeter by two times its height, you get PI to the fifteenth digit.

■ In 1980, a Las Vegas hospital suspended workers for betting on when patients would die.

PLACES

■ In Paris, the McDonalds big 'M' is the only one in the world that is white, rather than yellow; it was thought that yellow was too tacky.

■ In Washington DC no building can be built taller than the Washington Monument.

■ It is forbidden for aircraft to fly over the Taj Mahal.

■ Liberace Museum has a mirror-plated Rolls Royce, jewel-encrusted capes and the largest rhinestone in the world, weighing 59 pounds and measuring almost a foot in diameter.

■ Los Angeles's full name is El Pueblo de Nuestra Senora la Reina de los Angeles de Porciuncula – and can be abbreviated to 6.3 per cent of its size: LA.

■ Maine is the toothpick capital of the world.

PLACES

New York's Central Park is nearly twice the size of the entire country of Monaco.

New York's Central Park opened in 1876.

Printed on the book being held by the Statue of Liberty is 'July IV, MDCCLXXVI'.

Since the 1930's the town of Corona, California has lost all 17 of the time capsules they originally buried.

Some hotels in Las Vegas have gambling tables floating in their swimming pools.

The Angel Falls in Venezuela are nearly 20 times taller than Niagara Falls.

The blueprints for the Eiffel Tower covered more than 14,000 square feet of drafting paper.

PLACES

■ The clock at the National Bureau of Standards in Washington, DC will gain or lose only one second in 300 years because it uses cesium atoms.

■ The cost of building the Empire State Building was $40,948,900.

■ The Eiffel Tower has 2.5 million rivets.

■ The Eiffel Tower was built for the 1889 World's Fair.

■ The foundation of great European cathedrals go down as far as 40 or 50 feet.

■ The Future's Museum in Sweden contains a scale model of the solar system. The sun is 105 metres in diameter and the planets range from 5mm to 6km from the 'sun'. This particular model also contains the nearest star Proxima Centauri, still to scale, situated in the Museum of Victoria ... in Australia.

PLACES

■ The Golden Gate Bridge was first opened in 1937.

■ The Grand Canyon was not seen by a white man until after the Civil War. It was first entered on 29 May 1869 by the geologist John Wesley Powell.

■ The Great Wall stretches for 4,160 miles across North China.

■ The height of the Eiffel Tower varies as much as six inches depending on the temperature.

■ The highest motorway in England is the M62 Liverpool to Hull. At its peak it reaches 1,221 feet above sea level over the Saddleworth Moor (Greater Manchester), the burial ground of the victims of the infamous Myra Hindley, moors murderer.

■ The Hoover Dam was built to last 2,000 years. The concrete in it will not even be fully cured for another 500 years.

PLACES

■ The largest object that was ever found in the Los Angeles sewer system was a motorcycle.

■ The main library at Indiana University sinks over an inch every year because when it was built engineers failed to take into account the weight of all the books that would occupy the building.

■ The many sights that represent the Chinese city of Beijing were built by foreigners: the Forbidden City was built by the Mongols, the Temple of Heaven by the Manchurians.

■ The name of the woman on the Statue of Liberty is Mother of Exiles.

■ The names of the two stone lions in front of the New York Public Library are Patience and Fortitude. They were named by the then mayor Fiorello LaGuardia.

■ The nickname of Alcatraz Prison is 'The Rock'.

PLACES

The oldest university in the US is Harvard.

The Pentagon in Washington, DC has five sides, five storeys and five acres in the middle.

The proposed William Jefferson Clinton Presidential Library will have a section where you must be 18 or older to read certain documents.

The San Diego Zoo in California has the largest collection of animals in the world.

The San Francisco cable cars are the only mobile national monuments.

The shopping mall in Abbotsford, British Columbia, Canada has the largest water clock in North America.

The Statue of Liberty's mouth is three feet wide.

PLACES

The University of Alaska stretches over four time zones.

There are 102 floors in the Empire State Building.

There are 296 steps to the top of the Leaning Tower of Pisa.

There are 47 czars buried within the Kremlin.

There are 6,500 windows in the Empire State Building. There are more than 10 million bricks in the Empire State Building.

There are no clocks in Las Vegas gambling casinos.

There is a place in Norway called Hell.

There is a resort town in New Mexico called Truth or Consequences.

There is a town in Texas called Ding Dong.

PLACES

■ There is an airport in Calcutta named Dum Dum Airport.

■ There was once a town named '6' in West Virginia.

■ There were 57 countries involved in World War II.

■ There's a 'cemetery town' in California called Colma: its ratio of dead to living people is 750 to 1.

■ There's a bathroom in Egypt where it is free to use the toilet, but you have to bring/buy your own toilet paper.

■ Three Mile Island is only 2.5 miles long.

■ The Sphinx at Giza in Egypt is 240 feet long and carved out of limestone. Built by Pharaoh Khafre to guard the way to his pyramid, it has a lion's body and the ruler's head.

RELIGION

RELIGION

The Taj Mahal was actually built for use as a tomb.

The Taj Mahal was scheduled to be torn down in the 1830s.

■ A third of Taiwanese funeral processions include a stripper.

■ A young shepherd boy discovered the Dead Sea Scrolls at Qumram, Jordan, in 1947.

■ Almost all the villains in the Bible have red hair.

Christianity has over a billion followers. Islam is next in representation with half this number.

In ancient religions, the Norsemen considered the mistletoe a baleful plant that caused the death of Baldur, the shining god of youth.

RELIGION

■ In Turkey, the colour of mourning is violet. In most Muslim countries and in China it is white.

■ It was only after 440 AD that 25 December was celebrated as the birth date of Jesus Christ.

■ Kerimaki Church in Finland is the world's biggest church made of wood.

■ Las Vegas has the most chapels per capita than any other US city.

■ On the stone temples of Madura in southern India, there are more than 30 million carved images of gods and goddesses.

■ The election of a new pope is announced to the world with white smoke.

RELIGION

■ The first electric Christmas lights were created by a telephone company PBX installer. In the past, candles were used as light ornaments but they were dangerous, the installer took the lights from an old switchboard, connected them together, strung them on a tree and hooked them to a battery.

■ The last word in the Bible is Amen.

■ The longest chapter in the Bible is Psalm 119.

■ The practice of exchanging presents at Christmas originated with the Romans.

■ The three cardinal virtues are faith, hope and charity.

■ The youngest pope was 11 years old.

■ There are more than 1,700 references to gems and precious stones in the King James version of the Bible.

RELIGION

■ Two-thirds of Portugal was owned by the Church in the early eighteenth century.

■ Voodoo originated in Haiti.

■ Contrary to popular belief, there are almost no Buddhists in India, nor have there been for about a thousand years.

■ There's a temple in Sri Lanka dedicated to a tooth of the Buddha.

■ Though Buddhism was founded in India around 470 BC and developed there at an early date, it was uprooted from India between the seventh and twelfth centuries AD and today exists almost exclusively outside the country, primarily in Sri Lanka, Japan and Indochina.

■ Pope Adrian VI died after a fly got stuck in his throat as he was drinking from a water fountain.

RELIGION

■ Hindu men once believed it to be unluckily to marry a third time. They could avoid misfortune by marrying a tree first. The tree (his third wife) was then burned, freeing him to marry again.

■ Husbands and wives in India who desire children whisper their wish to the ear of a sacred cow.

■ According to ceremonial customs of Orthodox Judaism, it is officially sundown when you cannot tell the difference between a black thread and a red thread.

WORLD
OF SCIENCE

WORLD OF SCIENCE

The best working light-bulb a long time ago was a thread of sheep's wool coated with carbon.

107 incorrect medical procedures will be performed by the end of the day today.

5,280 feet make up one mile.

A Boeing 747's wingspan is longer than the Wright brothers' first flight.

A bolt of lightning can strike the earth with a force as great as 100 million volts.

A cesium atom in an atomic clock beats 9,192,631,770 times a second.

A creep is a metallurgical term for when something that is normally very strong bends because of gravity. This happens to many metals at high temperatures, where they won't melt but they will creep.

WORLD OF SCIENCE

■ A cubic mile of fog is made up of less than a gallon of water.

■ A device invented as a primitive steam engine by the Greek engineer Hero, about the time of the birth of Christ, is used today as a rotating lawn sprinkler.

■ A downburst is a downward blowing wind that sometimes comes blasting out of a thunderstorm. The damage looks like tornado damage, since the wind can be as strong as an F2 tornado, but debris is blown straight away from a point on the ground. It's not lifted into the air and transported downwind.

■ A fierce gust of wind blew 45-year-old Vittorio Luise's car into a river near Naples, Italy, in 1980. He managed to break a window, climb out and swim to shore, where a tree blew over and killed him.

WORLD OF SCIENCE

A fully loaded supertanker travelling at normal speed takes at least 20 minutes to stop.

A full moon always rises at sunset.

A full moon is nine times brighter than a half moon.

A jiffy is an actual unit of time for one-hundredth of a second. Thus the saying, 'I will be there in a jiffy!'

A jumbo jet uses 4,000 gallons of fuel to take off.

A large flawless emerald is worth more than a similarly large flawless diamond.

A lightning bolt generates temperatures five times hotter than those found on the sun's surface.

A manned rocket can reach the moon in less time than it took a stagecoach to travel the length of England.

WORLD OF SCIENCE

A metric mile is 1,500 metres.

A neutron star has such a powerful gravitational pull that it can spin on its axis in one-thirtieth of a second without tearing itself apart.

A normal raindrop falls at about seven miles per hour.

A pedometer measures walking distance.

A penny whistle has six finger holes.

A pulsar is a neutron star and it gets its energy from its rotation.

A rainbow can only occur when the sun is 40 degrees or less above the horizon.

The shell constitutes 12 per cent of an egg's weight.

A silicon chip a quarter-inch square has the capacity of the original 1949 ENIAC computer, which occupied a city block.

WORLD OF SCIENCE

A standard grave is 7'8 x 3'2 x 6'.

A syzygy occurs when three atronomical bodies line up.

A temperature of 70 million degrees Celsius was generated at Princeton University in 1978. This was during a fusionism experiment and is the highest man-made temperature ever.

A wind with a speed of 74 miles or more is designated a hurricane.

■ About seven million cars are junked each year in the US.

According to the Gemological Institute of America, up until 1896 in India was the only source for diamonds in the world.

According to the Texas Department of Transportation, one person is killed annually painting stripes on the state's highways and roads.

WORLD OF SCIENCE

All organic compounds contain carbon.

All snow crystals are hexagonal.

All the gold produced in the past 500 years, if melted, could be compressed into a 50-foot cube.

All the stars in our galaxy the Milky Way revolve around the centre of the galaxy every 200 million years.

All totalled, the sunlight that strikes earth at any given moment weighs as much as an ocean liner.

Almost all the helium that exists in the world today is from natural-gas wells in the United States.

American Airlines saved $40,000 in 1987 by eliminating one olive from each salad served in first class.

An enneahedron is solid with nine faces.

WORLD OF SCIENCE

■ An iceberg contains more heat than a match.

■ An inch of snow falling evenly on one acre of ground is equivalent to about 2,715 gallons of water.

■ Any free-moving liquid in outer space will form itself into a sphere because of its surface tension.

■ Approximately 98 per cent of software in China is pirated.

■ April is Earthquake Preparedness month. For a little added incentive, consider this: the most powerful earthquake to strike the United States occurred in 1811 in New Madrid, Missouri. The quake shook more than one million square miles, and was felt as far as 1,000 miles away.

■ Astronauts in orbit around the earth can see the wakes of ships.

WORLD OF SCIENCE

Astronomers classify stars by their spectra.

At any given time, there are 1,800 thunderstorms in progress over the earth's atmosphere.

At room temperature, the average air molecule travels at the speed of a rifle bullet.

Back in the mid to late 80s, an IBM-compatible computer wasn't considered a hundred per cent compatible unless it could run Microsoft's Flight Simulator.

Bacteria, the tiniest free-living cells, are so small that a single drop of liquid contains as many as 50 million of them.

Bamboo (the world's tallest grass) can grow up to 90cm in a day.

Because of the rotation of the earth, an object can be thrown further if it is thrown west.

WORLD OF SCIENCE

By weight, the sun is 70 per cent hydrogen, 28 per cent helium, 1.5 per cent carbon, nitrogen and oxygen, and 0.5 per cent all other elements.

Carolyn Shoemaker has discovered 32 comets and approximately 300 asteroids.

Chlorophyll makes plants green.

Clouds fly higher during the day than the night.

■ Construction workers hard hats were first invented and used in the building of the Hoover Dam in 1933.

Diamonds are composed of just one chemical element, carbon.

Did you know you share a birthday with at least nine other million people in the world?

DuPont is the world's largest chemical company.

WORLD OF SCIENCE

■ During the time that the atomic bomb was being hatched by the United States at Alamogordo, New Mexico, applicants for routine jobs like janitors were disqualified if they could read. Illiteracy was a job requirement. The reason: the authorities did not want their rubbish or other papers read.

■ Each year there is one ton of cement poured for each man, woman and child in the world.

■ Earth is travelling through space at 660,000 miles per hour.

■ Edmonton, Canada was the first city in North America with a population of less than one million to open a Light Rail Transit System in 1978.

■ Experts at Intel say that microprocessor speed will double every 18 months for at least 10 years.

WORLD OF SCIENCE

February 1865 is the only month in recorded history not to have a full moon.

Gold was the first metal to be discovered.

Hydrogen is the most common atom in the universe.

If you attempted to count the stars in a galaxy at a rate of one every second it would take around 3,000 years to count them all.

If you toss a penny 10,000 times it will not be heads 5,000 times but more like 4,950. The head picture weighs more, so it ends up on the bottom.

If you yelled for eight years, seven months and six days, you would have produced enough sound energy to heat one cup of coffee.

WORLD OF SCIENCE

■ In 1949, forecasting the relentless march of science, *Popular Mechanics* said computers in the future may weigh no more than five tons.

■ In 1961, MIT student Steve Russell, created SPACEWARS, the first interactive computer game, on a Digital PDP-1 (Programmed Data Processor-1) mainframe computer. Limited by the computer technology of the time, ASCII text characters were the 'graphics' and people could only play the game on a device that took up the floorspace of a small house.

■ India has the world's largest stock of privately hoarded gold.

■ India tested its first nuclear bomb in 1974.

■ Iron nails cannot be used in oak because the acid in the wood corrodes them.

WORLD OF SCIENCE

It takes eight and a half minutes for light to get from the sun to earth.

It takes one 15- 20-year-old tree to produce 700 paper grocery bags.

It takes the insect-eating Venus Flytrap plant only half a second to shut its trap on its prey.

Japan's currency is the most difficult to counterfeit.

Lab tests can detect traces of alcohol in urine six to 12 hours after a person has stopped drinking.

Life on earth probably developed in an oxygen-free atmosphere. Even today there are microorganisms that can live only in the absence of oxygen.

Man releases over a billion tons of pollutants into the earth's atmosphere every year.

WORLD OF SCIENCE

Mercury is the only metal that is liquid at room temperature.

Methane gas can often be seen bubbling up from the bottom of ponds. It is produced by the decomposition of dead plants and animals in the mud.

Moisture, not air, causes superglue to dry.

One ragweed plant can release as many as one billion grains of pollen.

A third of 95 developing countries have a waiting period of six years or more for a telephone connection, compared with less than a month in developed countries.

Orchids are grown from seeds so small that it would take 30,000 to weigh as much as one grain of wheat.

Recycling one glass jar saves enough energy to watch T V for three hours.

WORLD OF SCIENCE

Rene Descartes came up with the theory of co-ordinate geometry by looking at a fly walk across a tiled ceiling.

Robots in Japan pay union dues.

Russia built over 10,000 miles of railroad between 1896 and 1900.

The shortest intercontinental commercial flight in the world is from Gibraltar (Europe) to Tangier (Africa.) Distance: 34 miles; flight time: 20 minutes.

South Africa produces two-thirds of the world's gold.

Stainless steel was discovered by accident in 1913.

Stars come in different colours; hot stars give off blue light and the cooler stars give off red light.

WORLD OF SCIENCE

Sunbeams that shine down through clouds are called crepuscular rays.

The 'Big Bang' is said to have created the universe.

The Apollo 11 had only 20 seconds of fuel left when it landed.

The ashes of the metal magnesium are heavier than magnesium itself.

The average life of a nuclear plant is 40 years.

The bark of a redwood tree is fireproof. Fires that occur in a redwood forest take place inside the trees.

The billionth digit of PI is nine.

The Boeing 737 jet is nicknamed 'Fat Albert.'

The Boeing 747 has been in commercial service since 1970.

WORLD OF SCIENCE

The US Bureau of Standards says that the electron is the fastest thing in the world.

The CN Tower, in Toronto, is the tallest free-standing structure in the world.

The colour black is produced by the complete absorption of light rays.

The colour of diamond dust is black.

The company Kodak is the largest user of silver.

The condensed water vapour left by jets in the sky is called a contrail.

The densest substance on earth is the metal 'osmium.'

The external tank on the space shuttle is not painted.

The first American submarine was built around 1776.

WORLD OF SCIENCE

The first atomic bomb exploded at Trinity Site, New Mexico.

The first computer ever made was called ENIAC.

The first product Motorola started to develop was a record player for automobiles. At that time the most well-known player on the market was the Victrola, so they called themselves Motorola.

The leaves of the Victorian water lily are sometimes over six feet in diameter.

The metal instrument used in shoe stores to measure feet is called the Brannock device.

The metal part at the end of a pencil is 20 per cent sulphur.

The 111th element is known as unnilenilenium

WORLD OF SCIENCE

The process of splitting atoms is called fission.

The radio-active substance, Americanium-241 is used in many smoke detectors.

The Saguaro Cactus, found in the Southwestern United States, doesn't grow branches until it is 75 years old.

The Saturn V moon rocket consumed 15 tons of fuel per second.

The shockwave from a nitroglycerine explosion travels at 17,000 miles per hour.

The Siberian larch accounts for more than 20 per cent of all the world's trees.

The Sitka spruce is Britain's most commonly planted tree.

The smallest unit of time is the yoctosecond.

WORLD OF SCIENCE

The speed of sound must be exceeded to produce a sonic boom.

The strength of early lasers was measured in Gillettes, the number of blue razor blades a given beam could puncture.

The tail section of an airplane gives the bumpiest ride.

The tip of a bullwhip moves so fast that it breaks the sound barrier; the crack of the whip is actually a tiny sonic boom.

The total quantity of energy in the universe is constant.

The two hottest months at the equator are March and September.

The US standard railroad gauge (distance between rails) is 4 feet 8.5 inches.

The Venus flytrap can eat a whole cheeseburger.

WORLD OF SCIENCE

There are five tillion trillion atoms in one pound of iron.

Three astronauts manned each Apollo flight.

Three stars make up Orion's belt.

Toronto was the first city in the world with a computerized traffic signal system.

Twenty years make up a vicennial period.

When CBS broadcast the first television show in colour, no one other than CBS owned a colour television set.

When glass breaks, the cracks move at speeds up to 3,000 miles per hour.

You are most likely to lose your hearing than any of the other senses if you are hit by lightning.

SPORT

Anise is the scent on the artificial rabbit that is used in greyhound races.

A forfeited game in baseball is recorded as a 9–0 score. In American football it is recorded as a 1–0 score.

Australian Rules football was originally designed to give cricketers something to play during the off season.

Canada is the only country not to win a gold medal in the summer Olympic games while hosting the event.

Dartboards are made out of horse hairs.

Four men in the history of boxing have been knocked out in the first 11 seconds of the first round.

In 1936, American track star Jesse Owens beat a racehorse over a 100-yard course. The horse was given a head start.

SPORT

■ In the four professional major North American sports (baseball, basketball, football and hockey) there are only seven teams whose nicknames do not end with an S. These teams are the Miami Heat, the Utah Jazz, the Orlando Magic, the Boston Red Sox, the Chicago White Sox, the Colorado Avalanche, the Tampa Bay Lightning, and the Minnesota Wild.

■ In the United States, more Frisbee discs are sold each year than baseballs, basketballs, and footballs combined.

■ Kite flying is a professional sport in Thailand.

■ Morihei Ueshiba, founder of Aikido, once pinned a Sumo wrestler using only a single finger.

■ Nearly all Sumo wrestlers have flat feet and big bottoms.

■ Only two countries have participated in every modern Olympic Games, Greece and Australia.

SPORT

Pole vault poles used to be stiff. Now they bend which allows the vaulter to go much higher.

Rudyard Kipling, living in Vermont in the 1890s, invented the game of snow golf. He would paint his golf balls red so that they could be located in the snow.

Sports Illustrated has the largest sports magazine circulation.

Sprinters on track teams started taking a crouching start in 1908.

Ten events make up the decathlon.

The 1900 Olympics were held in Paris, France.

The 1912, Greco-Roman wrestling match in Stockholm between Finn Alfred Asikainen and Russian Martin Klein lasted more than 11 hours.

SPORT

■ The expression 'getting someone's goat' is based on the custom of keeping a goat in the stable with a racehorse as the horse's companion. The goat becomes a settling influence on the thoroughbred. If you owned a competing horse and were not above some dirty business, you could steal your rival's goat (seriously, it's been done) to upset the other horse and make it run a poor race. From goats and horses it was linguistically extended to people: in order to upset someone, get their goat.

■ The game of squash originated in the United Kingdom.

■ The national sport of Japan is sumo wrestling.

■ The only bone not broken so far during any ski accident is one located in the inner ear.

SPORT

There are at least two sports in which the team has to move backwards to win – tug of war and rowing.

There are six hoops on an Association croquet court.

Three consective strikes in bowling is called a turkey.

Tokyo has the world's biggest bowling alley.

Tug of war was an Olympic event between 1900 and 1920.

■ Badminton used to be called 'poona'.

Olympic badminton rules say that the birdie has to have exactly 14 feathers.

Fifty-six million people go to the Major League baseball each year.

A baseball has exactly 108 stitches.

SPORT

Babe Ruth wore a cabbage leaf under his hat to keep his head cool. He changed it every two innings.

Bank robber John Dillinger played professional baseball.

Baseball games between college teams have been played since the Civil War.

Baseball was the first sport to be pictured on the cover of *Sports Illustrated* magazine.

Baseball's home plate is 17 inches wide.

Before 1859, baseball umpires used to sit on rocking chairs behind the home plate.

It takes about eight seconds for a baseball bat to be made in a baseball bat factory.

The first formal rules for playing the sport of baseball required the winning team to score 21 runs.

SPORT

Basketball was invented by Canadian James Naismith in 1891.

Michael Jordan makes more money from Nike annually than all of the Nike factory workers in Malaysia combined.

Michael Jordan shaves his head on Tuesdays and Fridays.

The theme song of the Harlem Globetrotters is 'Sweet Georgia Brown'.

The bowling ball was invented in 1862.

Boxing is considered the easiest sport for gamblers to fix.

Boxing rings are called rings because they used to be round.

In 1985, Mike Tyson started boxing professionally at age 18.

The most popular sport as a topic for a film is boxing.

SPORT

- In the movie *Toy Story*, the carpet design in Sid's hallway is the same as the carpet design in *The Shining*.

- An American football has four seams.

- Green Bay Packers backup quarterback Matt Hasselbeck has been struck by lightning twice in his life.

- It takes 3,000 cows to supply the NFL with enough leather for a year's supply of footballs.

- OJ Simpson had a severe case of rickets and wore leg braces when he was a child.

- The Super Bowl is broadcast in 182 countries. That is more than 88 per cent of the countries in the world.

- When the University of Nebraska Cornhuskers play American football at home, the stadium becomes the state's third largest city.

SPORT

■ Americans spend more than $630 million a year on golf balls.

■ Before 1850, golf balls were made of leather and stuffed with feathers.

■ Fastest round of golf (18 holes) by a team was nine minutes and 28 seconds, set at Tatnuck CC in Worcester on 9 September 1996 at 10:40am.

■ Golfing great Ben Hogan's famous reply when asked how to improve one's game was: 'Hit the ball closer to the hole'.

■ In the US, there are more then 10,000 golf courses.

■ Many Japanese golfers carry hole-in-one insurance, because it is traditional in Japan to share one's good luck by sending gifts to all your friends when you get an ace. The price for what the Japanese term 'an albatross' can often reach $10,000.

SPORT

■ Pro golfer Wayne Levi was the first PGA pro to win a tournament using a coloured (orange) ball. He did it in the Hawaiian Open.

■ Someone constructs 12 new golf holes every day.

■ The only person ever to play golf on the moon was Alan Shepard. They never found the ball.

■ The Tom Thumb golf course was the first miniature golf course in the United States. It was built it 1929 in Chattanooga, Tennessee by John Garnet Carter.

■ The United States Golf Association (USGA) was founded in 1894 as the governing body of golf in the United States.

SPORT

■ The world's biggest bunker is Hell's Half Acre on the 535m 585yd seventh hole of the Pine Valley course, Clementon, NJ, built in 1912 and generally regarded as the world's most trying course.

■ The youngest golfer recorded to have shot a hole-in-one is Coby Orr (five years) of Littleton, CO on the 103yd fifth at the Riverside Golf Course, San Antonio, TX in 1975.

■ There are three golf balls sitting on the moon.

■ There are 336 dimples on a regulation golf ball.

■ A hockey puck is one inch thick.

■ Two golf clubs claim to be the first established in the United States: the Foxberg Golf Club, Clarion County, PA (1887) and St Andrews Golf Club of Yonkers, NY (1888).

SPORT

Canada imports about 850 Russian made hockey sticks on an average day.

Professional hockey players skate at average speeds of 20-25mph.

The city of Denver was chosen to host and then refused the 1976 Winter Olympics.

The five Olympic rings represent the continents.

Bulgaria was the only football team in the 1994 World Cup in which all the players, last names ended with the letters OV.

Football is played in more countries than any other sport.

Football legend Pele's real name is Edson Arantes do Nascimento.

■ The group Simply Red is named after its love for the football team, Manchester United who have a red home strip.

SPORT

■ A top freestyle swimmer achieves a speed of only four miles per hour. Fish in contrast, have been clocked at 68mph.

■ Captain Matthew Webb of England was the first to swim the English Channel using breaststroke.

■ Steffi Graf won her Grand Slam in tennis in 1988.

HISTORY 12

HISTORY

■ A 200-year-old piece of Tibetan cheese was auctioned off for $1,513 in 1993.

■ A B-25 bomber airplane crashed into the 79th floor of the Empire State Building on 28 July, 1945.

■ A golden razor removed from King Tut's tomb was still sharp enough to be used.

■ Abdul Kassam Ismael, Grand Vizier of Persia in the tenth century, carried his library with him wherever he went. The 117,000 volumes were carried by 400 camels trained to walk in alphabetical order.

■ According to the *Encyclopedia Britannica*, 11th Edition, from 1910 – 1911 the word toast was borrowed from the Old French *toste*, which has the Latin root of *torrere, tostum*, meaning to scorch or burn.

HISTORY

Acting was once considered evil, and actors in the first English play to be performed in America were arrested.

All of the officers in the Confederate Army were given copies of *Les Miserables* by Victor Hugo to carry with them at all times. Robert E. Lee, among others, believed that the book symbolized their cause. Both revolts were defeated.

All office seekers in the Roman empire were obliged to wear a certain white toga for a period of one year before the election.

Ancient Sybarites taught their horses to dance to music to make their parades more glamorous.

Any Russian man who wore a beard was required to pay a special tax during the time of Peter the Great.

HISTORY

■ At one point, the Panama Canal was going to be built in Nicaragua.

■ At the turn of the last millennium, Dublin had the largest slave market in the world, run by the Vikings.

■ Aztec emperor Montezuma had a nephew, Cuitlahac, whose name meant 'plenty of excrement'.

■ Before the 1800's there were no separately designed shoes for right and left feet.

■ In 1954 boxers and wrestlers had to swear under oath they were not communists before they could compete in the state of Indiana.

■ Children in the Chinook Indian tribe were strapped between boards from head to toe so that they would have fashionably flat skulls.

HISTORY

■ Close to 700,000 land mines were dug up from the banks of the Suez Canal after the 1973 war between Egypt and Israel.

■ Czar Paul I banished soldiers to Siberia for marching out of step.

■ Dinner guests during the medieval times in England were expected to bring their own knives to the table.

■ Dog Days: Days of great heat. The Romans called the hottest weeks of summer *canculares dies*. Their theory was that the Dog Star (Sirius), rising with the sun, added to its heat and the dog-days (about 3 July to 11 August) bore the combined heat of both.

■ In 18th – century France, visitors to the royal palace in Versailles were allowed to stand in a roped-off section of the main dining room and watch the king and queen eat.

HISTORY

■ During the American revolution, many brides used to wear the colour red instead of white as a symbol of rebellion.

■ During the Cambrian period, about 500 million years ago, a day was only 20.6 hours long.

■ During the Depression, banks first used sellotape to mend torn currency.

■ During the eighteenth century, books that were considered offensive were sometimes punished by being whipped.

■ During the Middle Ages, few people were able to read or write. The clergy were virtually the only ones that could.

■ During the Middle Ages, it was widely believed that men had one less rib than women. This is because of the story in the Bible that Eve had been created out of Adam's rib.

HISTORY

■ Eating chocolate was once considered a temptation of the devil.

■ Euripides was the first person on record to denounce slavery.

■ Everyone believed in the Middle Ages – as Aristotle had – that the heart was the seat of intelligence.

■ Evidence of shoemaking exists as early as 10,000 BC.

■ Francis Scott Key was a young lawyer who wrote the poem 'The Star Spangled Banner' after being inspired by watching the Americans fight off the British attack of Baltimore during the War of 1812. The poem became the words to the national anthem.

HISTORY

■ High-wire acts have been enjoyed since
the time of the ancient Greeks and
Romans. Antique medals have been
excavated from Greek islands depicting
men ascending inclined cords and
walking across ropes stretched
between cliffs. The Greeks called these
high-wire performers neurobates or
oribates. In the Roman city of
Herculaneum there is a fresco
representing an aerialist high on a rope,
dancing and playing a flute. Sometimes
Roman tightrope walkers stretched
cables between the tops of two
neighbouring hills and performed comic
dances and pantomimes while crossing.

■ If a family had two servants or less in
the US. in 1900, census takers recorded
it as lower middle-class.

■ If we had the same mortality rate as in
the 1900s, more than half the people in
the world today would not be alive.

HISTORY

In 1281, the Mongol army of Kublai Khan tried to invade Japan but were ravaged by a hurricane that destroyed their fleet.

In 1778, fashionable women of Paris never went out in blustery weather without a lightning rod attached to their hats.

In 1801, 20 per cent of the people in the US were slaves.

In 1900, the third leading cause of death was diarrhoea.

In 1917, Margaret Sanger was jailed for one month for establishing the first birth control clinic.

In 1937, yeast sales reached $20 million a year in the US.

In ancient Egypt, killing a cat was a crime punishable by death.

HISTORY

■ In certain parts of India and ancient China mouse meat was considered a delicacy.

■ In medieval England, beer was often served with breakfast.

■ In Puritan times, to be born on a Sunday was interpreted as a sign of great sin.

■ In the 1700s in London you could purchase insurance against going to hell.

■ In the 19th century, the British Navy attempted to dispel the superstition that Friday was an unlucky day to embark on a ship. The keel of a new ship was laid on a Friday; she was named HMS *Friday*, commanded by a Captain Friday and finally went to sea on a Friday. Neither the ship nor her crew were ever heard of again.

HISTORY

■ In the Great Fire of London in 1666, half of London was burned down but only six people were injured.

■ In the marriage ceremony of the ancient Inca Indians of Peru, the couple was considered officially wed when they took off their sandals and handed them to each other.

■ In Turkey, in the 16th and 17th centuries, anyone caught drinking coffee was put to death.

■ In Victorian times, there was an intense fear of being buried alive, so when someone died, a small hole was dug from the casket to the surface, then a string was tied around the dead person's finger which was then attached to a small but loud bell that was hung on the surface of the grave, so that if someone was buried alive, they could ring the bell and whoever was on duty would go and dig them up. Someone was on the duty 24 hours a day – hence the graveyard shift.

HISTORY

■ Income tax was first introduced in England in 1799 by British Prime Minister William Pitt.

■ Influenza caused over 20 million deaths in 1918.

■ It costs more to buy a car today than it cost Christopher Columbus to equip and undertake three voyages to the New World.

■ It has been calculated that in the last 3,500 years there have been only 230 years of peace throughout the civilized world.

■ It is estimated that within 20 years of Columbus discovering the New World the Spaniards killed off 1.5 million Indians.

■ Jaclyn Smith, Kate Jackson and Farrah Fawcett played the original Charlie's Angels.

■ Karate actually originated in India.

HISTORY

■ Leif Erikson was the first European to set foot in North America in the year 1000, NOT Columbus.

■ Long ago, the people of Nicaragua believed that if they threw beautiful young women into a volcano it would stop erupting.

■ Morocco was the first country to recognize the United States in 1789.

■ Native Americans never actually ate turkey; killing such a timid bird was thought to indicate laziness.

■ New Zealand was the first country to give woman the vote in 1890.

■ Olive oil was used for washing the body in the ancient Mediterranean world.

HISTORY

■ On 13 June 1944, a single Tiger tank headed by Cpt. Michael Wittman stopped the advance of the entire British 7th armoured division (the famous 'desert rats') in the town of Villers Bocage, Normandy. This had been the deadliest single action in the entire war and stopped the British offensive, planned by Montgomery, to break through German lines. Wittman died later in August fighting against 12 Canadian Sherman tanks.

■ Over 150 people were tried as witches and wizards in Salam, Massachusetts in the late 1600s.

■ Pilgrims ate popcorn at the first Thanksgiving dinner.

■ Pirates thought having an earring would improve their eyesight.

■ Pirates used weird nicknames to prevent government officials from identifying and persecuting their relatives back home.

HISTORY

■ Pope Paul IV, who was elected on 23 May 1555, was so outraged when he saw the naked bodies on the ceiling of the Sistene Chapel that he ordered Michelangelo to paint on to them.

■ Snow angels originated from medieval Jewish mystics who practised rolling in the snow to purge themselves from evil urges.

■ Spain declared war on the US in 1898.

■ Sumerians (from 5000 BC) thought that the liver made blood and the heart was the centre of thought.

■ The ancient Etruscans painted women white and men red in the wall paintings they used to decorate tombs.

■ *The Bird of Prey* was the name of the Wright brothers' first plane.

■ The Civil War was the first war in which news from the front was published within hours of its occurrence.

HISTORY

■ The earliest recorded case of a man giving up smoking was on 5 April, 1679, when Johan Katsu, Sheriff of Turku, Finland, wrote in his diary, 'I quit smoking tobacco.' He died one month later.

■ The eight-dollar bill was designed and printed by Benjamin Franklin for the American Colonies.

■ The first American in space was Alan B. Shepard Jr.

■ The origin of the most used four-letter word: in Irish police stations in the 19th century – when public indecency was a serious crime – couples were charged with being Found Under Carnal Knowledge. Police abbreviated it to its initials and called it a F U C K. charge.

■ The first man ever to set foot on Antarctica was John Davis on 7 February, 1821.

HISTORY

The first people to arrive on Iceland were Irish explorers in 795 AD.

The first police force was established in Paris in the year 1667.

The first telephone book ever issued contained only 50 names. It was published in New Haven, Connecticut, by the New Haven District Telephone Company in February 1878.

The guards of some of the emperors of Byzantium were Vikings.

The Hundred Years War lasted for 116 years.

The Indianapolis 500 is run on Memorial Day.

The Japanese anthem has the oldest lyrics/text from the ninth century, but the music is from 1880.

HISTORY

The Korean War began on 25 June, 1950.

The name of Charles Darwin's survey ship was *The Beagle*.

The name of the asteroid that was believed to have killed the dinosaurs was named Chixalub (pronounced Sheesh-uh-loob).

The Nobel Prize resulted from a late change in the will of Alfred Nobel, who did not want to be remembered after his death as a propagator of violence – he invented dynamite.

The Nobel Prize was first awarded in 1901.

The ruins of Troy are located in Turkey.

The shortest war in history was between Zanzibar and England in 1896. Zanzibar surrendered after 38 minutes.

HISTORY

- The Spanish Inquisition once condemned the entire Netherlands to death for heresy.

- The Toltecs, seventh-century native Mexicans, went to battle with wooden swords so as not to kill their enemies.

- There was a pony express in Persia many centuries before Christ. Riders on this ancient circuit, wearing special coloured headbands, delivered the mail across the vast stretch of Asia Minor, sometimes riding for hundreds of miles without a break.

- There were no ponies in the Pony Express.

- Those condemned to die by the axe in medieval and Renaissance England were obliged to tip their executioner to ensure that he would complete the job in one blow. In some executions, notably that of Mary, Queen of Scots, it took 15 whacks of the blade before the head was severed.

HISTORY

■ *Titanic* was running at 22 knots when she hit the iceberg.

To strengthen the Damascus sword, the blade was plunged into a slave.

Ukrainian monk Dionysius Exiguus created the modern day Christian calendar.

■ Until the Middle Ages, underwater divers near the Mediterranean coastline collected golden strands from the pen shell, which used the strands to hold itself in place. The strands were woven into a luxury textile and made into ladies' gloves so fine that a pair could be packed into an empty walnut shell.

Vikings used the skulls of their enemies as drinking vessels.

Welsh mercenary bowmen in the medieval period only wore one shoe at a time.

HISTORY

■ Westmount, Quebec, was the first city in Canada to be granted a coat of arms.

■ When Saigon fell the signal for all Americans to evacuate was Bing Crosby's 'White Christmas' being played on the radio.

■ When the *Titanic* sunk there was 7,500lbs of ham on it.

■ World Tourist Day is observed on 27 September.

■ Slaves under the last emperors of China wore pigtails so they could be picked out quickly.

■ The Chinese ideogram for 'trouble' depicts two women living under one roof.

HISTORY

■ The Chinese Nationalist Golf
Association claims the game is of
Chinese origin (ch'ui wan – the ball-
hitting game) in the third or second
century BC. There were official
ordinances prohibiting a ball game with
clubs in Belgium and Holland from
1360.

■ The Chinese, in historic times, used
marijuana only as a remedy for
dysentery.

■ The Great Wall of China, which is over
2,500 miles, took over 1,700 years to
build.

■ There is enough stone in the Great Wall
of China to build an eight-foot wall
encircling the globe at the equator.

■ Over half a million people died as a
result of the Spanish influenza
epidemic.

HISTORY

■ The sinking of the German vessel *Wilhelm Gustloff* is the greatest sea disaster of all time. Close to 8,000 people drowned.

■ About 300 years ago, most Egyptians died by the time they were 30.

■ According to the Greek historian Herodotus, Egyptian men never became bald. The reason for this, Herodotus claimed, was that as children Egyptian males had their heads shaved, and their scalps were continually exposed to the health-giving rays of the sun.

■ Ancient Egyptians shaved off their eyebrows to mourn the death of their cats.

■ Ancient Egyptians slept on pillows made of stone.

■ Cleopatra married two of her brothers.

HISTORY

■ Dead Egyptian noblewomen were given the special treatment of being allowed a few days to ripen, so that the embalmers wouldn't find them too attractive.

■ Egyptians once worshipped cats.

■ If a surgeon in ancient Egypt lost a patient while performing an operation, his hands were cut off.

■ In ancient Egypt, the apricot was called the egg of the sun.

■ In ancient Egypt, they paid their taxes in honey.

■ In Egypt, around 1500 BC. a shaved head was considered the ultimate in feminine beauty. Egyptian women removed every hair from their heads with special gold tweezers and polished their scalps to a high sheen with buffing cloths.

HISTORY

Moses Maimonides, 12th-century physician to the Egyptian Khalif, prescribed snow as a cure for the hot Cairo summers.

On some mummies that have been unwrapped, the total length of the bandages has been about 1.5 miles.

Preparing an Egyptian mummy sometimes took up to 70 days.

Ra was the sun god of ancient Egypt.

Ramses II, a pharaoh of Egypt died in 1225 BC. At the time of his death, he had fathered 111 sons and 67 daughters

The Egyptian city of Alexandria was discovered by Alexander the Great in 331 BC.

The Egyptian hieroglyph for 100,000 is a tadpole.

HISTORY

The first known contraceptive was crocodile dung, used by Egyptians in 2000 B.C.

Tomb robbers believed that knocking Eygptians sarcophagi's noses off would stall curses.

In English gambling dens, they used to have employees whose job was to swallow the dice if the police arrived.

Aphrodite was the Greek goddess of love.

Aristarchus was the first greek astronomer in 290 BC. to suggest that the sun was the centre of the solar system.

At the height of its power, in 400 BC, the Greek city of Sparta had 25,000 citizens and 500,000 slaves.

In ancient Greece, women counted their age from the date they were married.

HISTORY

■ Trivia is the Roman goddess of sorcery, hounds and the crossroads.

■ In ancient Japan public contests were held to see who in a town could break wind loudest and longest. Winners were awarded many prizes and received great acclaim.

■ There are 3,900 islands in the country Japan, the country of islands.

■ After the great fire of Rome in 64 AD, the emperor Nero ostensibly decided to lay the blame on Christians residing in the city of Rome. These he gathered together, crucified, covered in pitch (tar) and burned alive. He walked around his gardens admiring the view.

■ Ancient Romans believed that birds mated on 14 February.

■ Flamingo tongues were a common delicacy at Roman feasts.

HISTORY

■ Hannibal had only one eye after getting a disease while attacking Rome.

■ In ancient Rome, it was considered a sign of leadership to be born with a crooked nose.

■ In ancient Rome, weasels were used to catch mice.

■ It was decreed by law in the Roman Empire that all young maidens be fed rabbit meat because it would make them more beautiful and more willing.

■ Julius Caesar tried to beef up the population of Rome by offering rewards to couples who had many children.

■ Spartacus led the revolt of the Roman slaves and gladiators in 73 AD.

■ The Pantheon is the largest building from ancient Rome that survives intact.

HISTORY

■ The Roman emperor Caligula made his horse a senator.

■ The Roman emperor Commodos collected all the dwarfs, cripples and freaks he could find in the city of Rome and had them brought to the Colosseum, where they were ordered to fight each other to the death with meat cleavers.

■ The term 'It's all fun and games until someone loses an eye', is from ancient Rome. The only rule during wrestling matches was no eye gouging. Everything else was allowed but the only way to be disqualified was to poke someone's eyes out.

■ The year 2000 in Roman numerals is MM.

■ Each anchor chain link on the *Titanic* was about 175lbs.

■ The *Titanic* had four engines.

HISTORY

■ The *Titanic's* radio call sign was 'MGY'.

■ Two dogs were among the *Titanic* survivors.

■ During the First World War cigarettes were handed out to soldiers along with their rations.

■ During World War I, 13,700,000 people died in battle.

■ The first aerial photograph was taken from a balloon during the US Civil War.

■ A family of six died in Oregon during World War II as a result of a Japanese balloon bomb.

■ Corcoran Jump boots (army jump boots) have 82 stiches on the inside of the sole and 101 stitches on the outside of the sole in honour of the 82nd and 101st Airborne Divisions actions during World War II.

HISTORY

■ During conscription for World War II, there were nine documented cases of men with three testicles.

■ During World War II, it took the US only four days to build a ship.

■ During World War II, the Navajo language was used successfully as a code by the US.

■ During World War II, WC Fields kept US $50,000 in Germany 'in case the little bastard wins'.

■ During World War II, world champion chess player Reuben Fine helped the US calculate where enemy submarines might surface based on positional probability.

■ During World War II, Americans tried to train bats to drop bombs.

HISTORY

■ Escape maps, compasses and files were inserted into Monopoly game boards and smuggled into POW camps inside Germany during World War II; real money for escapees was slipped into the packs of Monopoly money.

■ 'John has a long moustache' was the coded signal used by the French Resistance in World War II to mobilize their forces once the Allies had landed on the Normandy beaches.

■ Kotex was first manufactured as bandages, during World War II.

■ Playing cards were issued to British pilots in World War II. If captured, they could be soaked in water and unfolded to reveal a map for escape.

■ Prior to World War II, when guards were posted at the fence, anyone could wander right up to the front door of the US President's residence the White House.

HISTORY

■ The first atomic bomb dropped on Japan fell from the *Enola Gay*, named after the unit commander's mother. The second was dropped from a plane known as Bock's Car.

■ The term 'the whole nine yards' came from World War II fighter pilots in the Pacific. When arming their planes on the ground, the .50-calibre machine gun ammo belts measured exactly 27 feet before being loaded into the fuselage. If the pilots fired all their ammo at a target, it got the whole nine yards.

■ The universally popular American Hershey bar was used overseas during World War II as currency.

■ The very first bomb dropped by the Allies on Berlin during World War II killed the only elephant in the Berlin Zoo.

HISTORY

■ World War II involved over 57 countries.

■ Ringo Starr was born during a World War II air raid.

STATISTICS

13

STATISTICS

■ One in 10 people are arrested every year in the US.

■ A car is stolen every 30 seconds in the United States.

■ Women shoplift more often than men; the statistics are four to one.

■ The longest kiss on record lasted 130 hours and two minutes.

■ The record for the world's worst driver is a toss-up between two candidates: first, a 75-year-old man who received 10 traffic tickets, drove on the wrong side of the road four times, committed four hit-and-run offences and caused six accidents, all within 20 minutes on 15 October, 1966. Second, a 62-year-old woman who failed her driving test 40 times before passing it in August 1970 (by that time, she had spent over £500 in lessons and could no longer afford to buy a car).

STATISTICS

The world record for carrying a milk bottle on your head is 24 miles.

0.3 per cent of all road accidents in Canada involve a moose.

One out of four people do not know what their astrological sign is.

Thirteen people a year are killed by vending machines falling on them.

Two and five are the only primes that end in two or five.

22,000 cheques will be deducted from the wrong bank accounts in the next hour.

Four per cent of the US population are vegetarians.

Forty per cent of women have hurled footwear at a man.

Fifty per cent of bank robberies take place on Fridays.

STATISTICS

Fifty per cent of teenage boys say that they would rather be rich than smart.

Fifty-one per cent of turns are right turns.

Fifty-five per cent of motorbike accidents happen on the weekend.

Fifty-six per cent of the video game market is adults.

Fifty-seven per cent of British school kids think Germany is the most boring country in Europe.

Sixty-nine per cent of men say that they would rather break up with a girl in private rather than in public.

Seven per cent of Americans think Elvis is alive.

Seventy per cent of all boats sold are used in fishing.

811,000 faulty rolls of 35mm film will be purchased this year.

STATISTICS

■ Eighty-two per cent of the world's population believe in an after life.

880,000 credit cards in circulation will turn out to have incorrect cardholder information on their magnetic strips.

Nine per cent of Americans have reported having been in the presence of a ghost.

Ninety per cent percent of women who walk into a department store immediately turn to the right.

Ninety-five per cent of food poisoning cases are never reported.

About one out of every 70 people who pick their nose actually eat their bogies.

About forty-three per cent of convicted criminals in the US are rearrested within a year of being released from prison.

STATISTICS

About five per cent of Americans claim to have talked to the devil personally.

About six per cent of murdered American men are killed by either their wife or girlfriend ... or wife who caught them with their girlfriend.

About 200 babies are born worldwide every minute.

Approximately 97.35618329 per cent of all statistics are made up.

Assuming Rudolph was in front, there are 40,320 ways to rearrange the other eight reindeer.

At 1.6 deaths for every 1,000 persons, Qatar has the lowest death rate in the world.

August is the month when most babies are born.

STATISTICS

Average age of top GM executives in 1994: 49.8 years. Average age of the Rolling Stones: 50.6.

Chances that a burglary in the US will be solved: one in seven.

Did you know that you're more likely to be killed by a champagne cork than a poisonous spider?

Experienced waitresses say that married men tip better than unmarried men.

Halifax, Nova Scotia, Canada has the largest number of bars per capita than anywhere else in the world.

In Calcutta, 79 per cent of the population live in one-room houses.

In Japan, 20 per cent of all publications sold are comic books.

In the next seven days, 800 Americans will be injured by their jewellery.

STATISTICS

It is estimated that at any one time, 0.7 per cent of the world's population are drunk.

It would take more than 150 years to drive a car to the sun.

Men are 1.6 times more likely to undergo by-pass surgery than women.

Meteorologists claim they're right 85 per cent of the time.

More people are killed by donkeys annually than are killed in plane crashes.

More than 10 per cent of all the salt produced annually in the world is used to de-ice American roads.

Most fatal car accidents happen on a Saturday.

Nobody yet has explained satisfactorily why couples who marry in January, February and March tend to have the highest divorce rates.

STATISTICS

Odds of being killed by a dog are one in 700,000.

Odds of being killed by a tornado are one in two million.

Odds of being killed by falling out of bed are one in two million.

Odds of being killed in a car crash are one in 5,000.

Odds of dying in the bathtub are one in one million.

Of the 266 men who have been pope, 33 have died violently.

On average, children between the ages of two and seven colour for 28 minutes every day.

One-quarter of the world's population lives on less than £140 a year. Ninety million people survive on less than £50 a year.

STATISTICS

Only 55 per cent of Americans know that the sun is a star.

Over 50 per cent of Americans believe in the devil.

Percentage of men who say they are happier after their divorce or separation: 58 per cent

Percentage of women who say they are happier after their divorce or separation: 85%

Pollsters say that 40 per cent of dog and cat owners carry pictures of their pets in their wallets.

Statistically the safest age of life is 10 years old.

Summer is statistically the most hazardous season.

Sweden has the least number of murders annually.

STATISTICS

Ten per cent of frequent fliers say they never check their luggage when flying.

The average adult spends about 12 minutes in the shower.

The average four-year-old child asks over 400 questions a day.

The average person keeps old magazines for 29 weeks before they throw them out.

The average person speaks about 31,500 words per day.

The average person spends about two years on the phone in a lifetime.

The average person will spend two weeks over their lifetime waiting for the traffic lights to change.

The murder rate in the United States is 200 times greater than in Japan. In Japan no private citizen can buy a handgun legally.

STATISTICS

The percentage of men who wash their hands after using a toilet is 55 per cent.

The percentage of women who wash their hands after using a toilet is 80 per cent.

Thirty-five per cent of the people who use personal ads for dating are already married.

Travelling by air is the safest means of transportation.

Twelve babies will be given to the wrong parents each day.

Two out of five husbands tell their wife daily that they love them.

You are more likely to get attacked by a cow than a shark.

Your statistical chance of being murdered is one in 20,000 thousand.

ODDS
AND ENDS

14

ODDS AND ENDS

■ A Virginia law requires all bathtubs to be kept out in the yards, not inside the house.

■ According to a British law passed in 1845, attempting to commit suicide was a capital offence. Offenders could be hanged for trying.

■ Christmas was once illegal in England.

■ Duelling is legal in Paraguay as long as both parties are registered blood donors.

■ George Washington is the only man whose birthday is a legal holiday in every state of the US as of a few years ago.

■ Impotence is legal grounds for divorce in 24 American states.

ODDS AND ENDS

■ In a tradition dating back to the beginning of the Westminster system of government, the bench in the middle of a Westminster parliament is two-and-a-half sword lengths long. This was so the government and oppositon couldn't have a go at each other if it all got a bit heated.

■ In Alaska it is illegal to shoot at a moose from the window of an aeroplane or other flying vehicle.

■ In Athens, Greece, a driver's licence can be taken away by law if the driver is deemed either 'unbathed' or 'poorly dressed'.

■ In Baltimore USA it is illegal to wash or scrub a sink regardless of how dirty it is.

■ In Cleveland, Ohio it is illegal to catch mice without a hunting licence.

ODDS AND ENDS

In England during Queen Victoria's reign, it was illegal to be a homosexual but not a lesbian. The reason being that when the Queen was approving the law she wouldn't believe that women would do that.

In Hartford, Connecticut, it is illegal for a husband to kiss his wife on Sundays.

In Helsinki, Finland, instead of giving parking tickets, the police usually deflate tyres.

In Italy, it is illegal to make coffins out of anything except nutshells or wood.

In Jasmine, Saskatchewan, it is illegal for a cow to moo within 300km of a private home.

In Kentucky, it is illegal to carry ice cream in your back pocket.

In Sweden, while prostitution is legal, it is illegal for anyone to use the services of a prostitute.

ODDS AND ENDS

In Texas, it is illegal to put graffiti on someone else's cow.

In the UK, there is no Act of Parliament making it illegal to commit murder. Murder is only illegal due to legal precedent.

It is against the law to stare at the mayor of Paris.

In Singapore, it is against the law to urinate in an elevator

In Sweden, it is illegal to train a seal to balance a ball on its nose.

In California, it is illegal to eat oranges while bathing.

In Bladworth, Saskatchewan, it is illegal to frown at cows.

It is illegal to grow or sell pork in Israel.

In Arizona, it is illegal to hunt camels.

ODDS AND ENDS

It is illegal, in Malaysia, for restaurants to substitute toilet paper as table napkins. Repeat offenders go to jail.

It used to be law in France that children's names had to be taken from an official government list.

In Iceland, it was once against the law to have a pet dog in a city.

In one city in Switzerland, it was once against the law to slam your car door.

Mailing an entire building has been illegal in the US since 1916 when a man mailed a 40,000-ton brick house across Utah to avoid high freight rates.

Pennsylvania was the first colony to legalize witchcraft.

A monkey was once tried and convicted for smoking a cigarette in South Bend, Indiana.

ODDS AND ENDS

According to the United States Refuse Act of 1899, every industrial discharge into bodies of water since 1899 has been a crime.

Every citizen of Kentucky is required by law to take a bath at least once a year.

If you live in Michigan, it is illegal to put a skunk in your boss's desk.

In Hartford, Connecticut, you may not, under any circumstances, cross the street walking on your hands.

In Idaho, a citizen is forbidden by law to give another citizen a box of candy that weighs more than 50 pounds.

In Indiana, it is illegal to ride public transportation for at least 30 minutes after eating garlic.

In Minnesota, it is illegal for woman to be dressed up as Santa Claus on city streets.

ODDS AND ENDS

In Morrisville, Pennsylvania, women need a legal permit before they can wear lipstick in public.

In some parts of Alabama, United States, it is illegal to carry a comb in your pocket.

In the 1985 Boise, Idaho, mayoral election, there were four write-in votes for Mr Potatohead.

In the Rhode Island legislature during the 1970s, it was proposed that their be a tax of $2 on every act of sexual intercourse.

In Oklahoma, it is against the law to hunt whale.

It is illegal for boys in 9th grade to grow a moustache in Binghamton, New York.

In a church in Omaha, Nebraska, it's against the law to burp or sneeze.

ODDS AND ENDS

■ In Kansas, it's against the law to catch fish with your bare hands.

It's against the law to ride down the streets of Brewton, Alabama, in a motorboat.

Most burglaries occur in the winter.

■ The state legislature in North Dakota has rejected a proposal to erect signs specifically warning motorists not to throw human waste on to the roadside. Maintenance workers report at least 20 incidents of road crews being sprayed with urine after rupturing urine-filled plastic bottles that became swollen in the hot sun. Opponents of the measure say they're afraid the signs would discourage tourism.

Under the law of Mississippi, there's no such thing as a female Peeping Tom.

There is a person in New Orleans with the name Luscious Pea.

ODDS AND ENDS

Abraham Lincoln's ghost is said to haunt the White House.

Adolf Hitler had planned to change the name of Berlin to Germania.

Adolf Hitler refused to shake Jesse Owens' hand at the 1936 Olympics because he was black.

Adolf Hitler was *Time*'s Man of the Year for 1938.

Al Capone's brother was a town sheriff.

Albert Einstein was offered the presidency of Israel in 1952.

Albert Einstein's last words were in German. Since the attending nurse did not understand German, his last words will never be known.

Alexander Graham Bell made a talking doll that said 'mama' when he was a young boy in Scotland.

ODDS AND ENDS

Alexander Graham Bell never telephoned his wife or mother. They were both deaf.

Alexander the Great was an epileptic.

Alexander the Great was tutored by Aristotle.

Alfred Hitchcock did not have a belly button.

American media mogul Ted Turner owns 5 per cent of New Mexico.

American explorer Richard Byrd once spent five months alone in Antarctica.

An eighteenth-century German named Matthew Birchinger, known as the little man of Nuremberg, played four musical instruments including the bagpipes, was an expert calligrapher and was the most famous stage magician of his day. He performed tricks with the cup and balls that have never been explained. Yet Birchinger had no hands, legs or thighs, and was less than 29 inches tall.

ODDS AND ENDS

Aristotle thought that blood cooled the brain.

Artist Constantino Brumidi fell from the dome of the US Capitol while painting a mural around the rim. He died four months later.

Astronaut Buzz Aldrin's mother's maiden name was 'Moon'.

Astronaut Neil Armstrong stepped on the moon with his left foot first.

At 12 years old, an African named Ernest Loftus made his first entry in his diary and continued everyday for 91 years.

At a fair in Maine, a boy spit a watermelon seed 38 feet.

At age 16, Confucius was a corn inspector.

ODDS AND ENDS

■ At age 47, the Rolling Stones' bassist, Bill Wyman, began a relationship with 13-year-old Mandy Smith, with her mother's blessing. Six years later, they were married, but the marriage only lasted a year. Not long after, Bill's 30-year-old son Stephen married Mandy's mother, age 46. That made Stephen a stepfather to his former stepmother. If Bill and Mandy had remained married, Stephen would have been his father's father-in-law and his own grandpa.

■ At age 90, Peter Mustafic of Botovo, Yugoslavia, suddenly began speaking again after a silence of 40 years. The Yugoslavian news agency quoted him as saying, 'I just didn't want to do military service, so I stopped speaking in 1920; then I got used to it'.

■ Attila the Hun was a dwarf. Pepin the Short, Aesop, Gregory the Tours, Charles III of Naples and the Pasha Hussain were all less than 3.5 feet tall.

ODDS AND ENDS

■ Augustus Caesar had achluophobia –
the fear of sitting in the dark.

■ Australian chemist John Macadamia
discovered the macadamia nut.

■ Benito Mussolini would ward off the
evil eye by touching his testicles.

■ Benjamin Franklin wanted the turkey,
not the eagle, to be the US national
symbol.

■ Benjamin Franklin was the first head of
the United States Post Office.

■ Benjamin Franklin's peers did not give
him the assignment of writing the
Declaration of Independence because
they feared that he would conceal a
joke in it.

■ Bill Gates's first business was Traff-O-
Data, a company that created machines
which recorded the number of cars
passing a given point on a road.

ODDS AND ENDS

British politician John Montagu, the 4t6h Earl of Sandwich, is credited with naming the sandwich. He developed the habit of eating beef between slices of toast so he could continue playing cards uninterrupted.

Buzz Aldrin was the first man to pee his pants on the moon.

Catherine de Medici was the first woman in Europe to use tobacco. She took it in a mixture of snuff.

Cathy Rigby is the only woman to pose nude for *Sports Illustrated*.

Charles de Gaulle's final words were 'It hurts'.

Charles Dickens never finished his schooling.

Charles Dickens was an insomniac, who believed his best chance of sleeping was in the centre of a bed facing directly north.

ODDS AND ENDS

Charlie Chaplin once won third prize in a Charlie Chaplin lookalike contest.

Christopher Columbus had blond hair.

Clark Gable used to shower more than four times a day.

Despite his great scientific and artistic achievement, Leonardo da Vinci was most proud of his ability to bend iron with his bare hands.

Dr Jekyll's first name is Henry.

Einstein couldn't speak fluently when he was nine. His parents thought he might be retarded.

Eleanor Roosevelt ate three chocolate-covered garlic balls every day for most of her adult life.

Eskimos never gamble.

ODDS AND ENDS

Euclid is known as 'The Father of Geometry'.

Every time Beethoven sat down to write music, he poured ice water over his head.

French astronomer Adrien Auzout once considered building a telescope that was 1,000 feet long in the 1600s. He thought the magnification would be so great he would see animals on the moon.

Galileo became totally blind just before his death. This is probably because of his constant gazing at the sun through his telescope.

Gandhi took dance and music lessons in his late teens.

Gandhi was born in 1869.

Genghis Khan started out as a goatherd.

ODDS AND ENDS

George Lucas's first movie was *THX 1138*, a thriller about a futuristic police state, filmed in 1971.

German chemist Hennig Brand discovered phosphorus while he was examining urine.

Hans Christian Anderson, creater of fairy tales, was word-blind. He never learned to spell correctly, and his publishers always had errors.

Harry Houdini was the first person to fly an airplane in the continent of Australia.

Harry Truman's middle name was just 'S'. It isn't short for anything. His parents could not decide between two different names beginning with S.

Henry Ford believed in reincarnation.

Henry Ford flatly stated that history is bunk.

Hitler and Napolean both had only one testicle.

ODDS AND ENDS

- Hitler was claustrophobic. The elevator leading to his Eagles' nest in the Austrian Alps was mirrored so it would appear larger and more open.

- Howard Hughes once made half a billion dollars in one day. In 1966, he received a bank draft for $546,549,171.00 in return for his 75 per cent holdings in TWA.

- Howdy Doody had 48 freckles.

- Howdy Doody's twin brother was Double Doody.

- Hrand Araklein, a Brink's car guard, was killed when $50,000 worth of quarters fell on and crushed him.

- Humphrey Bogart was related to Princess Diana, according to US genealogists.

- In 1911, Bobby Beach broke nearly all the bones in his body after surviving a barrel ride over Niagara Falls. Some time later in New Zealand, he slipped on a banana and died from the fall.

ODDS AND ENDS

In 1921, Albert Einstein was awarded the Nobel Prize for physics for his work with the photoelectric effect.

In 1968, a convention of beggars in Dacca, India, passed a resolution demanding that the minimum amount of alms be fixed at 15 paisa (three cents).

In 1976, a Los Angeles secretary named Jannene Swift officially married a 50-pound rock. The ceremony was witnessed by more than 20 people.

In 1982, the last member of a group of people who believed the earth was hollow died.

Isaac Newton dropped out of school when he was a teenager.

Isaac Newton used to be a Member of Parliament.

Issac Asimov is the only author to have a book in every Dewey-decimal category.

ODDS AND ENDS

Jacqueline Kennedy Onassis was the most famous editor at Doubleday & Co.

Jeremy Bentham, a British philosopher who died in 1832, left his entire estate to the London Hospital provided that his body preside over its board meetings. His skeleton was clothed and fitted with a wax mask of his face. It was present at the meeting for 92 years and can still be viewed there.

■ Jill St John, Jack Klugman, Diana Ross, Carol Burnett and Cher have all worn braces as adults.

John Bellavia has entered over 5,000 contests ... and never won anything.

John D Rockefeller was the first billionaire in the US.

■ John Hancock was the only one of 50 signatories of the Declaration of Independence who actually signed it in July.

ODDS AND ENDS

John Lennon's first girlfriend was named Thelma Pickles.

John Lennon's middle name was Winston.

John Quincy Adams took his last skinnydip in the Potomac on his 79th birthday.

John Travolta's *Saturday Night Fever* white suit was auctioned off for $145,500; Judy Garland's red slippers for $165,000; Charlie Chaplin's hat and cane for $211,500; Elvis's jacket for $59,700 and John Lennon's glasses for $25,875.

Julie Nixon, daughter of Richard Nixon, married David Eisenhower, grandson of Dwight Eisenhower.

Lee Harvey Oswald's body tag was auctioned off for $6,600.

Leon Trotsky, the seminal Russian Communist, was assassinated in Mexico with an icepick.

ODDS AND ENDS

■ Leonardo da Vinci could write with one hand and draw with the other at the same time.

■ Leonardo da Vinci invented the concept of the parachute, but his design was fatally flawed in that it did not allow air to pass through the top of the chute. Therefore, the chute would not fall straight, but would tilt to the side, lose its air and plummet.

■ Leonardo da Vinci invented the scissors.

■ Leonardo da Vinci spent 12 years painting the *Mona Lisa*'s lips.

■ Li Hung-chang is the father of Chop Suey.

■ Mae West was once dubbed 'The statue of Libido'.

■ 2 March is Dr Seuss's birthday.

ODDS AND ENDS

Marco Polo was born on the Croatian island of Korcula (pronounced Kor-Chu-La).

Marie Curie, the Nobel Prize-winning scientist who discovered radium, died on 4th July, 1934 of radiation poisoning.

Mark Twain was born in 1835 when Halley's comet appeared. He died in 1910 when Halley's comet returned.

Mel Blanc (the voice of Bugs Bunny) was allergic to carrots.

Michelangelo carved the famed Medici tombs in Florence.

More than 100 descendants of Johann Sebastian Bach have been cathedral organists.

Mozart is buried in an unmarked pauper's grave.

ODDS AND ENDS

Mozart wrote the nursery rhyme
'Twinkle Twinkle, Little Star' at the age
of five.

Mozart's real name was Johannes
Chrysostomus Wolfgangus Theophilus
Mozart.

Mr Mojo Risin is an anagram for
Jim Morrison.

Napoleon conducted his battle plans in
a sandbox.

Napoleon favoured mathematicians and
physical scientists but excluded
humanists from his circle, believing
them to be troublemakers.

Napoleon had his boots worn by
servants to break them in before he
wore them.

Napoleon Bonaparte was afraid of cats.

ODDS AND ENDS

■ Nobody knows where the body of Voltaire is. It was stolen in the nineteenth century and has never been recovered. The theft was discovered in 1864, when the tomb was opened and found empty.

■ Oliver Cromwell was hanged and decapitated two years after his death.

■ On a trip to the South Sea islands, French painter Paul Gauguin stopped off briefly in Central America, where he worked as a labourer on the Panama Canal.

■ Orson Welles is buried in an olive orchard on a ranch owned by his friend matador Antonio Ordonez in Sevilla, Spain.

■ Orville Wright was involved in the first aircraft accident. His passenger, a Frenchman, was killed.

■ Peter the Great executed his wife's lover and forced her to keep her lover's head in a jar of alcohol in her bedroom.

ODDS AND ENDS

■ Pluto, the astrological sign for death, was directly above Dallas, Texas when JFK was born.

■ Ralph Lauren's original name was Ralph Lifshitz.

■ Rita Moreno is the first and only entertainer to have received all four of America's top entertainment industry awards: the Oscar, the Emmy, the Tony and the Grammy.

■ Robert E. Lee wore size 4 ½ shoe.

■ Robert E. Lee, of the Confederate Army, remains the only person, to date, to have graduated from the West Point military academy without a single demerit.

■ Roger Ebert is the only film critic to have ever won the Pulitzer Prize.

ODDS AND ENDS

■ Russian IM Chisov survived a 21,980 feet plunge out of a plane with no parachute. He landed on the steep side of a snow-covered mountain.

■ Salvador Dali once arrived at an art exhibition in a limousine filled with turnips.

■ Samuel Clemens, aka Mark Twain, smoked 40 cigars a day for the last years of his life.

■ Sawney Beane, his wife, eight sons, six daughters and 32 grandchildren were a family of cannibals that lived in the caves near Galloway, Scotland in the early 17th century. Although the total number is not known, it is believed they claimed over 50 victims per year. The entire family was taken by an army detachment to Edinburgh and executed, apparently without trial.

■ Shakespeare spelled his own name several different ways.

ODDS AND ENDS

Sherlock Holmes's arch enemy was Professor Moriarty.

Sherlock Holmes had a smarter brother named Mycroft.

Sherlock Holmes never said, 'Elementary, my dear Watson'.

Sigmund Freud had a morbid fear of ferns.

Sir Issac Newton was an ordained priest in the Church of England.

Sir Issac Newton was only 23 years old when he discovered the law of universal gravitation.

Sister Boom-Boom was a transvestite nun who ran for mayor of San Francisco in 1982. He/she received over 20,000 votes.

Socrates committed suicide by drinking the poison hemlock.

ODDS AND ENDS

■ Socrates left no writings of his own.

■ Sophia Loren's sister was once married to the son of the Italian dictator Mussolini.

■ St Stephen is the patron saint of bricklayers.

■ Stalin's left foot had webbed toes, and his left arm was noticably shorter.

■ Susan Haswell Rowson was America's first bestselling novelist.

■ Telly Savalas and Louis Armstrong died on their birthdays.

■ The 16th-century astronomer Tycho Brahe lost his nose in a duel with one of his students over a mathematical computation. He wore a silver replacement nose for the rest of his life.

■ The first man to return safely from space was Yuri Gagarin.

ODDS AND ENDS

The German Kaiser Wilhelm II had a withered arm and often hid the fact by posing with his hand resting on a sword or by holding a glove.

The Mongol emperor Genghis Khan's original name was Temuji.

The Red Baron's real name was Manfred Von Richtofen.

The world record for most children to one mother is 69 children.

The world's youngest parents were eight and nine and lived in China in 1910.

■ There are about 15,000 people in the US over the age of 100.

There is a prison in Ossining, New York named 'Sing Sing'.

Thomas Edison had a collection of over 5,000 birds.

ODDS AND ENDS

Thomas Edison once saved a boy from the path of an oncoming locomotive.

Thomas Edison, the inventor of the lightbulb, was afraid of the dark.

Two sisters in the US, Susan and Deborah, weighed 205 and 124 pounds although they were only five and three years old respectively, in 1829.

Uri Geller, the professional psychic, was born in 1946. As to the origin of his alleged powers, Mr Geller maintains that they come from a distant planet of Hoova.

Valentina Tereshkova was the first woman to enter space.

Vincent Van Gogh comitted suicide while painting *Wheat Field with Crows*.

Vincent Van Gogh decided to become an artist when he was 27 years old.

Walt Disney died of lung cancer.

ODDS AND ENDS

■ Walt Disney's autograph bears no resemblance to the famous Disney logo.

■ Warren Beatty and Shirley MacLaine are brother and sister.

■ When Beethoven was a child, he made such a poor impression on his music teachers that he was pronounced hopeless as a composer.

■ When Einstein was inducted as an American, he attended the ceremony without socks.

■ When John Wilkes Booth leaped on to the stage after shooting the President, he tripped on the American flag.

■ When Patty Hearst was kidnapped, she was watching the TV show *The Magician* starring Bill Bixby.

■ When young and impoverished, Pablo Picasso kept warm by burning his own paintings.

ODDS AND ENDS

◼ Winston Churchill was born in a ladies' room during a dance.

◼ Wonder Woman has yellow stars all over her blue shorts.

◼ World heavyweight boxing champion, Gene Tunney also lectured on Shakespeare at Yale University later in his life.

◼ Worldwide there are more statues of Joan of Arc than of anyone else. France alone has about 40,000 of them.

◼ Writer Director Actor Albert Brooks's real name is Albert Einstein.

◼ Writer Edgar Allan Poe and LSD advocate Timothy Leary were both kicked out of West Point.